AF580021

Pennsylvania German Illuminated Manuscripts

Pennsylvania German Illuminated Manuscripts

A Classification of Fraktur-Schriften

and An Inquiry into their History and Art

Henry S. Borneman

WITH REPRODUCTIONS IN COLOR

Dover Publications, Inc., New York

Published in Canada by General Publishing Company, Ltd., 30 Lesmill Road, Don Mills, Toronto, Ontario.
Published in the United Kingdom by Constable and Company, Ltd., 10 Orange Street, London WC 2.

This Dover edition, first published in 1973, is a corrected republication of the work originally published in 1937 by the Pennsylvania German Society as Volume 46 of its Proceedings and Papers.

International Standard Book Number: 0-486-22926-2
Library of Congress Catalog Card Number: 72-95048

Manufactured in the United States of America
Dover Publications, Inc.
180 Varick Street
New York, N. Y. 10014

DEDICATED TO

Ralph Beaver Strassburger, LL.D.

TO WHOM EVERY DESCENDANT

OF THE

PENNSYLVANIA GERMAN PIONEERS

IS A DEBTOR

Preface

THE printer gives the Preface first place in the book. But the Author writes his preface last. After the text has been written, there remain a lot of odds and ends of appreciation and desire whose vitality has persisted. These matters cry to be put into print although they may not be of general interest, and perhaps should be omitted. The customary use of the Preface, however, enables the author, without embarrassment, to say certain things about himself and his effort, with the idea of establishing pleasant relations between himself and his hoped for reader.

Let it be said at once, therefore, that the pronoun I will be used without further ado about the matter. The abandonment of third-person and impersonal references will save printers' ink and the residuum of egotism will neither be increased nor diminished thereby.

My grandmother, Esther Latshaw Stauffer, was born in 1789 and even at that early date in the history of the United States she was the grand-daughter of a German ancestor who had settled in Pennsylvania almost seven decades before her birth. Prior to her death at the age of over ninety, she gave to me a manuscript belonging to the class which forms the subject of this monograph. Hence my first expression of appreciation is due to my grand-mother; for the giving of that fragment of paper, with its hallowed associations, developed an intense and enjoyable quest to collect and study Pennsylvania German manuscripts.

For more than five decades that bit of manuscript has drawn to itself a large collection of companions—an abomination to a good and tolerant housekeeper but a perennial joy to me. The reproductions in color in this publication are taken in their entirety from my collection in the hope that intensive studies will be made by those who have acccss to othcr collcctions.

I appreciate my indebtedness to many antique dealers who knew my weakness. As to the pecuniary end of our relations, they must thank me. But I remain indebted to them and thank them for many bits of information which on their part were subconscious leaks of salesmanship by means of which avenues of inexhaustible research were opened to me.

It is greatly to be regretted that Pennsylvania German Manuscripts have not been collected and preserved by Historical Societies, excepting the notable collection in the Schwenkfelder Library at Pennsburg, Pennsylvania. Where specimens of these manuscripts have appeared, they are usually put on display as relics or curios and their historical and art values are overlooked. This lack of source material accessible to the public, partly accounts for many thin and hastily drawn conclusions regarding the emotional ability of the Pennsylvania German to produce and appreciate the aesthetic or the beautiful—call it art, if you please.

The absence of available collections suggested the idea of reproducing in color a representative number of these manuscripts; for no amount of descriptive writing can give an adequate notion of their beauty of design, richness of color, or their aesthetic or art value.

The reader will find that the text of this monograph is a mere outline of the subject matter. This is due to lack of space but it may be a fortunate prohibition. A pleasing text of literary merit easily weaves itself into a scarlet cloak, often covering two cardinal sins of omission in historical writing—laziness in research and negligence in verifying statements of fact.

Of course, I am indebted to many authors whose works entered into the preparation of this monograph and there has been a strong temptation to annex a Bibliography. But space will be saved and a more helpful service rendered the interested reader by merely calling his attention to the fact that exhaustive Bibliographies are to be found in the books cited in the text.

Henry S. Borneman

Overbrook, Philadelphia
March 22, 1937.

Table of Contents

List of Plates

Pennsylvania German Illuminated Manuscripts

Pennsylvania Germans

(*Pennsylvanische-Deutsche*)

IN former days titles of books, both English and German, were verbose and frequently they almost became a table of contents. The first book printed by Christopher Sauer in 1739 is an apt illustration. It was a hymnal used by the Brotherhood at Ephrata, Pennsylvania, and it is usually referred to by two words, in its title, viz.: *Weyrauchs Hugel.* On the title page, however, there are twenty-two lines of printing with a total of one hundred words.

Fashions among modern printers demand that the title shall be brief and that it shall convey a fair idea of the nature of the subject matter. *Pennsylvania German Illuminated Manuscripts,* the title of this monograph, adopted after mature deliberation, immediately presents two questions:—Who are the Pennsylvania Germans? What are illuminated manuscripts?

The reader's attention is invited to the first question. After Columbus had opened a new route of adventure, the colonization of America was undertaken nationally by Spain, England, Holland, France and Sweden. In a governmental sense, no attempt to establish an American colony was made by the small sovereignties, together spoken of as Germany. It is, however, a striking fact that in those early days thousands upon thousands of Germans, individually and in family and community groups, moved by the spirit of adventure and hope, settled in various American Colonies—in Pennsylvania, New Jersey, New York, Maryland, Louisiana, Maine, Virginia, Georgia and the Carolinas.

The horrors of war, oppression by the civil authorities, and persecution by religious zealots, are commonly given as the reasons for the abandonment of their native land and the adoption of new abodes ruled by nations, foreign to them and to which they became bound through oaths of allegiance. These vicissitudes as proximate causes of emigration, moreover, were inflicted upon a people in whom, when opportunity offered, the spirit of the pioneer was strong—that same spirit which in subsequent years drove them to reclaim virgin soil in the western portion of the United States and in Canada, far removed from the original port of entry in America.

One illustration will show how they kept pace with a rapidly growing nation. Matthias Gish arrived in the Port of Philadelphia in 1733. To revere his memory his descendants have organized "The National Association of the Gish Family of America." They have active State Associations in Ohio, Indiana, Nebraska, Minnesota, Oregon and California. There are Regional or Local Associations in other States as follows:—Virginia, Kentucky, Illinois, Kansas, Michigan, Wisconsin, Colorado, Nebraska, Iowa, Oregon, Texas and West Virginia.

William J. Hinke, in *Pennsylvania German Pioneers* says that the first ship, bringing Germans in large numbers, of which a record has survived, was the ship "America," which landed at Philadelphia August 20, 1683. Francis Daniel Pastorius was the leader of the group which settled in Germantown, Pennsylvania. Tides of German immigration succeeded each other during the century following. The names of about 40,000 who arrived in Philadelphia between 1727 and 1808 appear in documents in the Archives of Pennsylvania and are recorded in print in *Pennsylvania German Pioneers*, just referred to. A clearer idea of the large number of arrivals may be obtained from a statement made by Dr. Hinke to the effect that the total number of ships arriving at the Port of Philadelphia between 1727 and 1775 is 324 and that they carried approximately 65,000 German passengers.

Records were not kept of the particular places from which they came. The Captains of the ships, in their carelessly prepared lists of passengers, generally described them as Palatines. A comparative study of the German dialects which they spoke, has enabled philologists to locate the places of their origin with exceeding particularity. William Dwight Whitney in *The Life and Growth of Language* (New York 1875) says:

> "When the ethnological relations of a community or of a group of communities are to be settled, the first question is as to the affinities of its speech. This does not necessarily decide the case; the linguistic evidence may be overborne by some other; but nothing can be determined without it; it lays the basis for further discussion. We need only to quote an example or two in illustration of this. . . . Of the Etruscans there are records and descriptions and pictures, and products, art and industrial; but to settle the relationship of the race the ethnologists with one consent appeal to the infinitesimal remnants of Etruscan speech: a single page of connected Etruscan text, with but a hint of its meaning, would in the briefest time settle the question whether the race is to be connected with any other on earth, or whether, like the Basque, it is an isolated fragment."

S. S. Haldeman in a treatise entitled *Pennsylvania Dutch* (Philadelphia 1872) finds that these Pioneers brought their speech from the Upper Rhine and the Neckar, the latter furnishing the Suabian or Rhenish Bavarian element and that it is South German and to be found in Rhenish Bavaria, Baden, Alsace (Alsatia), Württemberg, German Switzerland and Darmstadt.

Marion Dexter Learned in *The Pennsylvania German Dialect* (Baltimore 1887) ascribes the origin of the dialects to the Lower Rhine, near Düsseldorf, Suabian border; Rhine Palatinate, Alsace-Lorraine, Switzerland, Silesia, Moravia.

Marcus Bachman Lambert in *A Dictionary of the Non-English Words of the Pennsylvania German Dialect* (1923) points us to Southwestern Germany (the Palatinate, Baden, Alsace, Württemberg, Hesse), Saxony, Silesia and Switzerland.

Oscar Kuhns in *The German and Swiss Settlements of Colonial Pennsylvania* (New York 1901) puts the place of the origin of the dialect in the States of South Germany, the three principal of which were Palatinate, Württemberg and Switzerland; and in Silesia and Moravia.

Thus philology establishes the particular duchy, electorate, principality or political sovereignty (collectively referred to as Germany) as the place of origin and labels the racial group. These Pioneers and their descendants very properly referred to themselves as Pennsylvanische Deitsche (High German, Deutsch). This their English neighbors translated into the term Pennsylvania-Dutch as a convenient out-of-mouth translation without intending to define nationality. Pennsylvania-German is, however, truly descriptive of their ethnic origin, for their homeland was, almost entirely, Germany and not Holland, at the time of their emigration.

Interesting as the pursuit may be, it is not necessary to go further into ethnological origins. Our immediate purpose rather requires a consideration of the status of the Pennsylvania Germans from the standpoint of their associated community lives, particularly in the land of their adoption.

One by one the original German Pioneers in Pennsylvania passed to their long home. They had felled the trees of the forest. They had reclaimed the soil for tillage. Barns for storage of hay and fodder and buildings for horses and cattle had been built. Houses in which centered the family life had been constructed. In a generation or two direct contact with the Fatherland had been severed and the German group whom we now call the Pennsylvania Germans had become an integral part of the American community. Their condition was not an unhappy one. The soil yielded sustenance. The hand of the Government rested lightly upon their shoulders. Their religious faith and practice was unrestrained. With a slight modification, they had reached the ideal of William Morris (magnetic Master-Craftsman and Socialist after his own order) as expressed by him in his *Roots of the Mountains*:

"Thus then lived this folk in much plenty and ease of life, though not delicately or desiring things out of measure. They wrought with their hands, and wearied themselves; and they rested from their toil and were merry; tomorrow was not a burden to them, nor yesterday a thing which they would fain forget: life shamed them not, nor did death make them afraid."

Those early settlers are generally thought of only as farmers and supporting occupations are overlooked. But the farmer had to be housed and sheltered and fed. He had affection for his wife and children. He had religious faith and the hope of a happy state after life's end. The necessities of life, the cravings of the mind, and the longings of the spirit were not to be turned up by the plough or reaped by the sickle. Shelter required carpenters, masons and builders. Clothing necessitated fullers, weavers, and tailors. Farming could not be carried on without blacksmiths, saddlers and wheelwrights. The housewife engaged the services of the miller, potter and cabinet-maker.

The aspirations of the mind and the cravings of the spirit called for the employment of the schoolmaster and the clergyman, and their work was quickened by the erection of paper mills and the operation of printing presses.

Thus there were developed artisans and craftsmen of great skill whose products are cherished heirlooms to this day and the quest of modern collectors.

In those early days, the most effective advertising lay in the skill of fine performance. That aroused the desire to outdo his fellow artisans and competition arose. The moment competition begins, the road to excellence opens. Thus the craftsman applied aesthetic principles in his work. Builders constructed rural dwellings with lines pleasing even to the eye of the modern architect. Workers in iron applied beauty of design to their hinges, locks, lamps, kettles and implements for the hearth. Cabinet-makers became notable craftsmen in the construction of furniture. Potters aimed for beauty of form, color and glaze. The schoolmaster strove for excellence in penmanship and through the use of decorative designs, heightened with brilliant colors, he produced manuscripts of great beauty.

Illuminated Manuscripts
(*Fraktur-Schriften*)

IT is desirable that the first definition should be an ocular one—such as may be obtained if the reader will examine the facsimile reproductions of the Pennsylvania German Illuminated Manuscripts reproduced in this book. The primary impression so obtained will be aided by a few verbal definitions. Subsequent sections will deal with the purposes, production, history and other features of these manuscripts.

Writing is the art or act of tracing or setting down letters, words or graphic signs, adapted for reading or recording by hand, on paper, parchment or other material, with a pen, pencil, style brush or other instrument.

A *Manuscript* (manus, hand; scriptus, to write) means a book, document or the like in writing; or a writing of any kind as distinguished from print. (See *Oxford Dictionary.*)

To *Illuminate* is to decorate an initial-letter, word or text in a manuscript, with gold, silver, or brilliant colors or with elaborate tracery and miniature designs executed in colors. (*Oxford Dictionary.*) J. H. Middleton in *Illuminated Manuscripts in Classical and Medieval Times* (Cambridge 1892) says:

> "The medieval phrase *illuminated manuscript* means a manuscript which is *lighted up* with colored decoration in the form of ornamental initial-letters or painted miniatures. Dante speaks of the art which in Paris is called *illuminating.*"

By applying the relevant parts of the foregoing definitions to the manuscripts here being considered and adding the statement that they were made by Pennsylvania Germans, we have naturally arrived at a definition of Pennsylvania German Illuminated Manuscripts, without the necessity of further verbiage. They may properly be referred to as *Fraktur-Schriften* (Fraktur-writings). This term will be discussed in the section dealing with the designs appearing in these manuscripts.

The practice of the art of illumination by the Pennsylvania Germans was a survival and a revival of the art firmly established in the Middle Ages before the invention of printing. An understanding of the art at its height is necessary to appreciate the survival in its deeper phases. Let us look briefly at the early history and development of the art.

Many books dealing with the subject of Illuminated Manuscripts have been published. Most of them are out of print and not readily obtainable. There is a present need and place for an authoritative treatise, with a text flowing from the pen of a ready writer, with reproductions in color of typical manuscripts and obtainable at prices that are not prohibitive. In the meantime the following treatises will likely be found in good libraries:

Illuminated Manuscripts by John W. Bradley (Chicago 1909)
The Art of Illuminating by M. D. Wyatt and Tymms (London 1860)
Das Schriftwesen im Mittelalter by W. Wattenbach (Leipzig 1875)
The Art of Illumination as Practised in the Middle Ages by Henry Shaw (London 1866)
Illuminated Manuscripts in Classical and Medieval Times by J. H. Middleton (Cambridge 1892)
The Book of Kells by Edward Sullivan (The Studio, London 1914)
Die Deutsche Buchmalerei by Franz Jacoby (Munich 1923)

The art of illumination in Western Europe has its origin among the Celtic people residing in what is now known as Ireland. I once made a never-to-be-forgotten visit to the Library of Trinity College in Dublin, Ireland, for the express purpose of seeing the illuminated manuscript known as the *Book of Kells*, the most ancient and typical specimen of the Celtic calligraphers. The manuscript is ascribed to the sixth or seventh century and its name was derived from the fact that it belonged to the ancient Monastery of Cennanus or Kells, which is generally asserted to have been erected by St. Columba about A. D. 550. Columba was known as Collum Cille, i. e., Columb of the Church (b. 521—d. 597).

The Book of Kells has had an interesting history which cannot be recited here. The text deals with the four Gospels. From the artistic standpoint, the design and development of initial letters is of striking prominence and indeed, the treatment of the initial is at the very foundation of occidental manuscripts. The details consist of designs and borders of intertwined bands or ribbons, twisted knots, spirals, dragons, serpents and legendary animals, executed with marvelous dexterity.

Before the year 1000, this style of illumination had been carried by the Irish Missionaries to the Island of Iona off the Scottish coast; to the Monasteries of Lindisfarne and Glastonbury in England; and St. Boniface, the great awakener of Germany to Christianity, had carried with him a highly ornamented Book of the Gospels. Evidences of the transmission of Celtic art by the zealous missionaries of the early Church in Ireland also appear in the books of St. Kilgin, the Apostle of Franconia, in books preserved at the Monastery of St. Gall in Switzerland; and even in Italy at the Monastery at Bobbio.

In a general study of the art of illumination, it is helpful to remember that the manuscripts of Western Europe had art forms which were primarily designed and developed in the West through the centuries; and that when designs of oriental or other character appear they had to filter through the sieve of occidental form and design. The West was not a servile copyist of the East and where traces of foreign art appear, they were the product of assimilated influences seasoned by time.

In an address on *Decorative Colour*, delivered in 1854, John Ruskin states that the main idea which prevailed during the Middle Ages was that "a book was a noble and a sacred thing to be respected and revered. It became precious because it was written with so much labor and with so much beauty; and then came the idea of its sanctity. It was noble inasmuch as it was the means of making human thought—the most transient and evanescent of all things—the most permanent of all things." In support of this view, Ruskin read an anecdote respecting an eminent calligrapher who lived in the time of Charlemagne, as follows:

> "There was in the monastery of Arnisberg a writer named Richard, an Englishman, who had with his own hand copied a great number of books, hoping to receive in heaven a recompense for his labours. When he quitted this life his brother monks buried him in a place of honour. Twenty years afterwards his tomb was opened, and his right hand was found in as perfect a state of preservation as though it were alive, and appeared to have been recently cut off from an animated body, while all the rest of the corpse was dust. This hand is shown as a great miracle to this day in the monastery of Arnisberg."

In the *Chronicon Ephratense* (Ephrata, Pennsylvania 1786) it is recorded that some members of the Cloister spent years in the writing-school and that it served as a means of sanctification to crucify their flesh (auf dem heiligungs-weg zur creutzigung der natur).

In *Das Leben und Wandel* (Ephrata, Pa. 1825) Ezechiel Sangmeister records that upon becoming a Brother in the Ephrata Cloister, he had great difficulty in finding a worthy occupation leading to a higher life. Conrad Beisel, the leader of the group, advised him to learn to sing by note, to engage in writing in fraktur and to color designs. These very material occupations did not satisfy Sangmeister's intense desire for the higher life, and he then gave himself over to prayer, spending hours at a time on bended knee for Divine guidance. The spiritual but very practical Beisel, however, from time to time assigned him such tasks as carpenter work, singing, "Frakturschreiben," and designing of pictures.

No one has more keenly or more beautifully portrayed the sacredness attached to the art of illumination in the Middle Ages and to the sense of spiritual responsibility of those engaged in its practice than Henry Wadsworth Longfellow. In his poem entitled *The Golden Legend*, one of the scenes is laid in the Convent of Hirschau in the Black Forest, and is as follows:

The Scriptorium

FRIAR PACIFICUS *transcribing and illuminating*

FRIAR PACIFICUS:

It is growing dark! Yet one line more,
And then my work for to-day is o'er.
I come again to the name of the Lord!
Ere I that awful name record,
That is spoken so lightly among men,
Let me pause awhile, and wash my pen;
Pure from blemish and blot must it be
When it writes that word of mystery!

Thus have I labored on and on,
Nearly through the Gospel of John.
Can it be that from the lips
Of this same gentle Evangelist,
That Christ himself perhaps has kissed,
Came the dread Apocalypse?
It has a very awful look,
As it stands there at the end of the book,
Like the sun in an eclipse.

Ah me! when I think of that vision divine,
Think of writing it, line by line,
I stand in awe of the terrible curse,
Like the trump of doom, in the closing verse!
God forgive me, if ever I
Take aught from the book of that Prophecy,
Lest my part too should be taken away
From the Book of Life on the Judgment Day.

This is well written, though I say it!
I should not be afraid to display it,
In open day, on the selfsame shelf
With the writings of St. Thecla herself,
Or of Theodosius, who of old
Wrote the Gospels in letters of gold!
That goodly folio standing yonder,
Without a single blot or blunder,
Would not bear away the palm from mine,
If we should compare them line for line.

There, now, is an initial letter!
Saint Ulric himself never made a better!
Finished down to the leaf and the snail,
Down to the eyes on the peacock's tail!
And now, as I turn the volume over,
And see what lies between cover and cover,
What treasures of art these pages hold,
All ablaze with crimson and gold,
God forgive me! I seem to feel
A certain satisfaction steal
Into my heart, and into my brain,
As if my talent had not lain
Wrapped in a napkin, and all in vain.

Yes, I might almost say to the Lord,
Here is a copy of thy Word,
Written out with much toil and pain;
Take it, O Lord, and let it be
As something I have done for thee!

[*He looks from the window.*]

How sweet the air is! How fair the scene!
I wish I had as lovely a green
To paint my landscapes and my leaves!
How the swallows twitter under the eaves!
There, now, there is one in her nest;
I can just catch a glimpse of her head and breast,
And will sketch her thus, in her quiet nook,
For the margin of my Gospel book.

[*He makes a sketch*]

William Morris is authority for the statement that at the beginning of the Thirteenth Century "a sundering of the styles of different peoples begins to be obvious"; and that by the close of the century a complete differentiation between the work of the countries of Europe was to be noted and three great schools of illumination had developed: The French-Flemish-English; the Italian; and the German.

The art began its decline when the laity began to supplement the work of the ecclesiastics. The adoption by Gutenberg and other Germans of the art of printing by means of movable type in the middle of the Fifteenth Century was the final cause of the rapid disintegration of the art of the calligrapher and illuminator and when the German emigration to America began, the glorious day of the illuminated manuscript had ended. This art had a history of more than a thousand years during which thirty generations had lived and died and naturally several centuries had to elapse before the art had spent itself. The last notable practice of illumination (even though it be a mere fragment of its highest development) is to be found among the Pennsylvania Germans, among whom it had a conspicuous place in religious, educational and social life for a hundred years. In 1897 Henry C. Mercer, a great philosophical antiquarian, delivered an address which he very properly entitled: "*The survival of the mediaeval art of illuminative writing among the Pennsylvania Germans.*" The brief address, covering eleven pages, is based upon honest research and has remained, to this day, as the only authoritative treatment of the subject. (See Proceedings of American Philosophical Society, Vol. xxxvi; No. 156. Also publication of Bucks County, Pa., Historical Society).

A Forward Look

MORE than three hundred Pennsylvania German Illuminated Manuscripts of all sorts and sizes have crowded themselves into the portfolios of my collection. These manuscripts are generally referred to as *Fraktur-Schriften.* Let us examine them in the abstract for the purpose of classification, in order that we may see what place they shall have in the text of this monograph.

First of all, we have a class which distinctively belongs to the schoolmaster and the schoolroom, and which served as specimens of the schoolmaster's ability to handle the pen and the brush and, in part, as copying exercises for his scholars. These manuscripts are known as *Vorschriften.*

The scholars, of course, had to learn their A B C's, and this brings to the fore manuscripts which corresponded to a primer and were frequently known as *Das Guldene A B C.*

For excellence in work the scholar had to receive an award of some sort and this frequently took the form of an attractive free-hand design, a bit of color-work, or a certificate of merit. These are in the class known as a *Belohnungen* or *Prizes.*

In their family relationships, genealogy occupied a prominent place. Records were made of births, marriages and deaths in the Family Bible and in single page manuscripts. In this class are placed the *Geburtschein* and the *Trauschein.*

In religious life, we find certificates of baptism or christening, certificates of confirmation, and manuscripts whose general purpose was to present a Biblical text or moral precept in an attractive form. In this group of manuscripts, are included the *Taufschein*, the *Irrgarten* and *Die Sieben Reglen der Weisheit* and other manuscripts whose purpose was the teaching of religious and moral truth.

The house as a place of residence was regarded as sacred and the blessing of God was invoked as appears in the manuscripts referred to as the *Haus-Segen.*

The foregoing list presents a general survey of the treatment of the text so far as the purposes of the manuscripts are concerned. In addition to that there will be sections dealing with the penman himself; his quill and brush; his inks and pigments; his paper and other necessary materials. Reference will also be made to the revival of producing illuminated manuscripts as folk art; showing its distribution and chronology. There will now be considered in detail the several classes just referred to.

Specimen of Calligraphy (*Vorschrift*)

Reward of Merit (*Belohnung*)

Primer (*Guldene A B C*)

Vorschriften, Belohnungen, and *Das Guldene A B C* are manuscripts which belong to the School-master and the School. They will be considered together in this section which will largely have to do with the youth.

THE primary definition of the word *Vorschrift* suggests a writing set as a pattern or specimen to be copied or followed. It brings to mind the Copy-books in use in the ungraded schools a half century ago. What a time the scholars had as they, with pen in hand, strove to acquire excellence in the art of penmanship by laboriously filling page after page with imitations of the printed specimen at the top of each page. These Copy-books, in Spencerian or other forms, had a worthy predecessor in the Copy-book made, about 1820, by Carl Frederich Egelman, a notable engraver who resided in Berks County, Pennsylvania. His publication bore the following title:

> "Deutsche & Englische Vorschriften für die Yugend. Aufgesetzt und gestochen von Carl Frederich Egelman."

The book has twelve copper-plates, each being five and one-half by seven inches in size. Each plate is beautifully engraved. Here are the letters of the alphabet in various forms—Kleines-Alphabet; Groszes-Alphabet; Alten-Schriften; Fraktur-Alphabet; Englisches oder Lateinisches Alphabet and Numerals. On one page we find a school-room beautifully engraved on copper in stipple. At a table is seated the school-master and a paper is being handed him by a boy who has just entered through the open door. In another part of the room, near a shelf, full of books, a boy is seated at another table engaged in writing. On either side of the school-room, there is engraved a scene out-of-doors with trees, birds, windmills. Below the picture appears, beautifully engraved in German and English, the following instruction to the young:

> From art and study true content must flow
> For 'tis a God-like attribute to know
> He most improves who studies with delight
> And learns sound morals while he learns to write.

Printed copy-books were, of course, not in use in early days. Manuscript exercises for the practice of penmanship by pupils in school were supplied by the school-master. In my possession is an interesting copy-book with the following inscription on the first page, surrounded with a yellow border in which are circles in red: *Dieses Schreib-Büchlein gehöret Rebecca Berckholder zu.* It is dated November 25, 1828. It is a booklet consisting of six leaflets—two by seven and one-half inches in size. On the twelve small pages there are letters and Bible quotations in script and seven precepts in carefully written Gothic fraktur letters, among them, in translation, being the following:

> Often read your book, so you may become wise.
> A child that does not learn, will remain ignorant.
> Tell not all you know for that is foolishness.
> Serve God in thy youth.

Vorschriften, as specimens of hand-writing to be imitated and *Belohnungen* (rewards of merit), are intimately associated with the educational program of the Pennsylvania Germans. The education of the youth in early days was a matter closely allied with the Church —Church and School went hand in hand. The School-master frequently was a lay-teacher of the Church. He often met his pupils in the Church building or in a separate school building close by.

James P. Wickersham in *A History of Education in Pennsylvania* (Lancaster 1891) may be consulted for details relating to this interesting subject.

Instruction was given in the three R's, often referred to as "Readin', Ritin' and 'Rithmetic." Anyone familiar with the teaching in early Pennsylvania German schools will add two additional R's—Religion and Rhythm. In those days the McGuffy and the Sanderson Readers were unknown. The Bible was the text-book used in the teaching of reading. That, however, was not its only use. The School-master adopted it for the major purpose of giving Religious instruction to the pupil. The schools were the hand-maid of the Church. The schools were opened and closed with prayer (See *Deutsche Schul-Gebäte zum gebrauch für Amerikanische Schulen zum anfang und ende derselben.* Northampton, Gedruckt bey Henrich Ebner, 1815).

The additional R, to which I refer, was the teaching of Rhythm through singing. Schools were opened and closed with singing. Singing was taught in the schools to the children and it was a social custom in the community to conduct so-called "Singing Schools" among those beyond school age. Plate No. 27 shows a reward of merit (*Belohnung* or *Preis*) for "the best singer in the second class."

The School-master was thus charged with the teaching of Reading, Writing, Arithmetic, Religion and Singing.

It is well known that especial attention was given to the teaching of writing. To be a good penman was a valued accomplishment and a very essential qualification for the School-master to have. He showed his skill in the manuscripts known as Vorschriften. They may be understood as being specimens of his skill in writing; as being exercises in calligraphy to be copied; or as samples of handwriting, design and decoration.

The enlarged use of the word *vorschrift,* beyond that of being a mere copying-exercise, is shown by referring to *Muhlenberg and Schipper's English-German Dictionary* (Lancaster 1812) where German equivalents of the word *copy* are the following: "Abschrift, nachschrift, handschrift, vorschrift, das exemplar."

Plate No. 3 very properly labels, not only itself, but all manuscripts of this class in these words:

> "Vorschrift der Liebhabern zum Lesen und Schreiben"
> (Specimen writing for those who desire to read and write).

As to contents, the Vorschriften have the same general form. Usually a verse from the Bible, or some moral precept, is used for the purposes of the display of especial skill in designing Gothic fraktur letters and in the application of colors. This is followed with further quotations from the Bible, a hymn or moral precepts in script. At the close we find, in script, the letters of the alphabet in capitals and lower case; followed with the numerals from one to ten. In some cases there are musical scores for the hymn.

These hand-produced specimens in calligraphy and decoration, particularly with their religious matter, in Gothic black letter and script, followed with the letters of the alphabet and the ten numerals, remind one of the old Horn-Books in use, especially in England.

The Horn-book consisted of a board with a handle—in the shape of a paddle. On one side a piece of transparent horn was attached so as to leave a space between the board and the horn. A sheet of paper was inserted into the open space and through the transparent horn the pupil read the printed matter which usually consisted of the letters of the alphabet, the numerals, the Lord's prayer or possibly a scripture text.

The poet William Cowper in his *Tirocinium or a Review of the Schools* (1784) thus describes a Horn-Book:

"Neatly secured from being soiled or torn
Beneath a pane of thin transparent horn,
A book (to please us at a tender age
'Tis called a book, though but a single page)
Presents the prayer the Savior deign'd to teach,
Which children use, and parsons—when they preach."

Andrew W. Toner in his *History of the Horn-Book* (London 1897) says that the Horn-Book was in use in Germany but that there is no equivalent for that word in German.

Whether Horn-Books were used in Pennsylvania does not clearly appear. Alice Morse Earle noted an advertisement in the *Pennsylvania Gazette*, for December 4, 1760, for the sale of Bibles and primers with "gift horns and plain horns," which she says "were certainly Horn-books."

Specimens of Horn-Books are rare. In the pride of possession (a trait with which collectors are curiously affected) I may say that I have a specimen made of leather with the ten numerals and a cross in red on the back. Because it is made of leather, I suppose some technically informed collector will tell me that it is spurious.

I do not wish to be understood as saying that Vorschriften were Horn-Books. I have resurrected this ancient matter for the purpose of contrasting methods of teaching in earlier days.

The statement that Vorschriften and Belohnungen had to do with schools and school-masters must remind those who know Pennsylvania German history of Christopher Dock—"the pious Schoolmaster on the Skippack." He was born in Germany at a date unknown. Omitting the few known details of his life, the thought of the reader is directed to his work as the teacher of schools in Germantown, Philadelphia, and in Skippack and Salford Townships, Montgomery County, Pennsylvania. In 1750 he wrote a treatise on school-management which was published by Christopher Saur in 1770. It consisted of an octave pamphlet of fifty-four pages and its main title is *Schul-Ordnung*.

It is not within our present aims to deal with Dock's pedagogical methods in detail. His general purpose was to reward excellence rather than punish delinquency. Progress deserves reward. Thus when the pupil had learned his a, b, c's, his father owed him a penny and his mother must fry him two eggs for his diligence; and such reward (belohnung) must also be given him when the pupil has reached the name stage. When he begins to read then the master himself issues a certificate of merit (*Zeugnisz*). If there is lack of progress, the pupil was assigned to another pupil as a monitor who receives for his service *eine vorschrift oder vogel*—a writing-copy or specimen, or a bird. A record was kept of merits attained during the day and the master was indebted to the one having the highest number of credits—a flower or a bird drawn on paper (*solchen bin ich auch etwas schuldich, etwa eine Blum auf papier gemahlet oder einen Vogel*). The pupils were given an hour for lunch. To guard against misusing their freedom, one or two of the pupils were engaged to read portions of the Old Testament to the rest during which time the master was writing: (*so lang ich ihnen vorschreibe*).

Dock composed hymns which were used in the Mennonite Congregations. This will again be referred to. These he taught to his pupils and sang Psalms with them (*also habe ich dann auch Lieder und Psalmen mit ihnen gesungen, weilen von beyden theilen, als nehmlich, von geistreichen Liedern und Psalmen, der Heilige Geist der Werckmeister*).

Dock's views on education, religious teachings, moral precepts, and hymns occasionally appeared in *Ein Geistliches Magazien* which Christopher Saur began to publish in Germantown, Pennsylvania, in 1764. It is said to be the first religious periodical published in America. It appeared at irregular times until 1774. A complete set of fifty issues in the first part and of fifteen issues in the second part lies before me as this is being written and is rarely met with.

Authenticated manuscripts by Christopher Dock are very rare. In Martin G. Brumbaugh's *Life and Works of Christopher Dock* there are reproductions in half-tone only, some of which represent Dock's penmanship. Dock's handwriting may be seen in his will (signed "Christopher Durk") which is on file in the Office of the Register of Wills in Philadelphia (Will No. 116 of 1771). The late Howard W. Kriebel (for whom a memorial should be established in recognition of his valuable contributions to Pennsylvania German history) was for many years engaged in a search for Dock manuscripts. He called my attention to the will of John Fried registered in the office of the Register of Wills of Philadelphia in Will Book G page 160. To that will Dock is a subscribing witness, he having signed it in the name of "Christoph Dock." Both wills are in English and evidently are specimens of Dock's penmanship.

Christopher Dock was an outstanding teacher in pioneer days. His statement of principles of pedagogy was among the first in America. From his school-room went those who practiced the art of illumination and helped to continue it as folk art. A sketch of his life will be found in the *Dictionary of American Biography.*

The vorschrift reproduced as Plate No. 21 came to me through Rev. Nathaniel B. Grubb, who has been my much esteemed friend for over fifty years. Family tradition has it that it was given by Dock to his pupil Mary Steiner who later was married to Abraham Clemens.

A comparison of the handwriting as it appears in the two wills above referred to with the reproduction of the vorschrift on page 248 of Brumbaugh's *Life of Dock*, and with the original manuscript herein produced as Plate No. 21, leads to the inescapable conclusion that all of these manuscripts were written by Dock.

Dock also used *Das Guldene A B C* as a means of teaching, not only reading but also religion. The learning of the letters of the alphabet must have been an experience of major dimensions. It seems to have been taught by means of an arrangement of the letters of the alphabet successively; each letter beginning a text of scripture; or the first letter of the subject of a sentence conveying a moral precept. The immediate task was to learn the letters of the alphabet but the harder task was the committing to memory of moral precepts and Biblical texts. As an illustration of this there is the arrangement of the letters appearing in the well known *Guldene A B C* (The Golden A B C). A copy may be found on page 248 of Brumbaugh's *Life of Christopher Dock*, above referred to, in which scripture texts are used. At a later date large broadsides of the *Guldene A B C* were printed. Each of the twenty-five German letters (one less than the English alphabet) has a verse of four lines.

A very interesting specimen, in manuscript, in the A B C form, bears the searching title of: *Wilt du bald ein Doctor Werden?* (1796) (Do you wish to become a Doctor without great effort?).

The process of becoming a Doctor without great effort, lies in knowing the alphabet and its implications and is set forth in a manuscript by Jacob Beidelman dated March 14, 1796. The text is as follows:

Wilt du bald ein Doctor werden

Ohne grosse muhe kanst du alle kunst auf erden das dir's fehlet nie. Das heiszt viel in wenig stunden in dem A B C gefunden, wie du siehest hie.

A sull alle ding verlassen
B Bosheit spricht das B
C das creuz mit freuden fassen
D Demut gibt das D
E fuehrt in das ewig leben
F die freud dem herzen geben

G Gedult gibt das G.
H geburt heilig zu leben
I inbrustig seyn
K Kon kurtze worte geben
L lieb Gott allein
M soll massig seyn und bleyben
N mit nutz die ziet vertreiben
O Ohn falschheit seyn
P die pflicht der lieb zu achtern
Q soll quahlen seyn
R nach reinen hertzen trachten
S mit sanft-muth seyn
T soll tugend andre lehren
U soll untertaenig hoeren
W soll wachtsam seyn

Der bluehend schoene May
Der frusched yugend yahren
Is so geschwind verbei
Zu ewigkeit gefahren
Drum somlei blumlei ein

Kanst du die buchstaben nicht alle sagen
Auf ein mahl, will ich dir den inhalt sagen:

Liebe Gott allein
Fasse dieses recht zusammen
Tief ins hartze hinein
Hast dieses recht verstanden
So kannst du in allen landen
der beste Doctor sein.

Birth Certificate (*Geburts-Schein*)
Baptismal Certificate (*Tauf-Schein*)
Wedding Certificate (*Trau-Schein*)
Family Record (*Familien Register*)

Birth, Baptismal and Wedding Certificates will be considered in this section. Being of the same class as to substance, reference will also be made to genealogical records in Bibles or elsewhere.

THE manuscripts relating to birth and baptism are not, as a class, certificates in the technical sense of that term. A certificate, as generally understood, is a writing, which serves as evidence of a matter of fact, and it is signed by a public official or by one familiar with the facts whose truth is vouched for. Very rarely, indeed, do these Pennsylvania German manuscripts have the name of a person certifying to its truth. They were, however, accepted as verity and reasons therefor readily suggest themselves. The very form of the manuscript carried with it a certification of truth. A skilled calligrapher was not employed to make a manuscript with pleasing letters, designs, decorations and color to record an untruth. Then, too, it was carefully preserved for posterity and the statements were accepted as being true in the family groups and thus these manuscripts acquired the credential value of a formal certificate.

In earlier days, when births were not recorded in public offices, records were privately kept and the most frequent and most authoritative place of record in general use, was the large family Bible, together with records in hymnals, and other books of a religious nature. These were often engrossed by a skilled penman. Of course, the Baptismal certificates always have the record of birth. So at times do Book-plates and other genealogical manuscripts.

The manuscript record of Johannes Meurer before 1800 shows the birth of nine children, the signs of the Zodiac for each being indicated. It was a common practice to have the date of birth followed with a reference to the sign of the Zodiac. In a Book-plate in a Hymnal of German Reformed Church it is written that Maria Staufer was born April 8, 1777, *im Zeichen des wieders* (in the sign of the ram).

It was the practice of the illuminators of Books of Hours during the Middle Ages to indicate in the calendar representations of the signs of the Zodiac. The well-known "anatomy man" in the old almanacs was accompanied with the signs of the Zodiac. This custom has an ancient origin. Grillot DeGivry in *Witchcraft, Magic and Alchemy* (Boston 1931) recalls that the ancients, in the midst of the heaven of the fixed stars, had established the existence of seven mobile celestial bodies which they called the planets, viz.: the Sun, the Moon, Mercury, Venus, Mars, Jupiter and Saturn. These they marked with traditional symbols, which were used in the old almanacs. The *moon* is the "planet" of brooding and melancholy. *Mercury* is the planet of commerce and the arts. The *sun* presides over glory and earthly riches. *Mars* rules war and battles. *Jupiter* has to do with honors and physical beauty. *Saturn* foretells accidents, violent deaths and disasters. The author also states:

> "Among the fixed constellations the ancients had ascertained twelve groups of stars, in which they had discovered the sun rose above the horizon successively during the full course of a year; these twelve constellations formed a broad band or girdle, called the Zodiac, in the celestial sphere. They too are

distinguished by traditional symbols." Their names and corresponding signs are as follows:

Ram	♈	Lion	♌	Archer	♐
Bull	♉	Virgin	♍	Goat	♑
Twins	♊	Scales	♎	Water-carrier	♒
Crab	♋	Scorpion	♏	Fishes	♓

"The angular distances from time to time subsisting between the planets in the celestial vault are called 'aspects'; the interpretation of these aspects forms the basis of astrology. . . . The whole of celestial space is divided into twelve parts called houses; each part includes thirty degrees of the Zodiac and corresponds to a particular phase of human life.

"In order to interpret a horoscope it is necessary to know the influences of the seven planets, the twelve signs of the Zodiac, the astrological houses and of the various aspects of the planets and their position in the different signs of the Zodiac. It is very difficult to form a conception of the resulting complications unless one has practiced the art. . . . Astrology gained such credit among men of all peoples of the world that it was the only branch of occult science which the church dared not formally condemn. In reading all the Fathers and doctors of the Church, from St. Augustine to St. Thomas Aquinas, it is perceptible that their teaching on this subject is hesitant. They disapprove without completely rejecting."

In a very rare German incunabulum, *Martyrologium der Heillegen nach dem Kalender* printed at Strasbourg by Johann Pruss in 1484, there is a wood-cut in which the localization of the signs of the Zodiac to the various parts of the human body clearly appear. This is a significant early appearance of the "Anatomy man" so well known to readers of early almanacs, whether in German or English.

In view of these ancient customs, and in view of the difficulties attending the practice of astrology, the reader is allowed to make his own guess as to what was in the mind of a Pennsylvania German when he read his birth certificate which recorded the fact of his birth in one of the signs of the Zodiac.

The form of Illuminated Manuscript most frequently met which is the *Tauf-Schein* or *Baptismal Certificate*. This form has persisted even to the present day. It passed rapidly out of its manuscript-form into a printed certificate, with blanks for names and dates to be filled in by a competent scribe. Even before 1800, certificates were printed with borders, in outline, of birds, flowers and other decorative designs which were then filled in by hand in color. They are very commonly met with and many of the decorations are poorly done and lack artistic merit. At later dates certificates were printed in color by Kohler of Philadelphia, Ritter of Allentown, Peters of Harrisburg, Currier and Ives, Bauman of Ephrata, Stover of Lebanon, Krebs of Reading and others.

It is to be expected that the Baptismal certificates are to be found among the religious groups practicing infant baptism. The certificate was an expression of love for childhood by the parents and it was a record of the fact of baptism which became vital when the child appeared for confirmation later in life.

These certificates, like the birth certificates already referred to, were very rarely signed. But they acquired their evidential value for the reasons already referred to. The genealogical value of the Baptismal certificates cannot be overemphasized because of the facts usually recorded. Following the name of the child are the names of father and mother, with her maiden name; the date of birth, the place of birth, usually the Township and County being given; the name of the officiating clergyman, with a frequent reference to his denomination; and the names of the witnesses present. Thus we have a document giving exact family names; their places of residence at a definite date; the connection and place of service of the officiating clergyman and additional names of the family or friends living in that locality.

As has been said the printed and inartistically decorated certificates are very plentiful and, as a rule, they may be purchased at low prices. I was offered seventy-two certificates at twenty-five cents a piece recently—a most attractive price but not yielded to because I am not pursuing genealogical research. It is greatly to be regretted that a movement has not been started to buy up all these certificates for their very great genealogical value. Some Historical Society should undertake such collecting. The amount of money involved or needed would be comparatively small.

Plate No. 14 is the reproduction of a manuscript *Geburts und Taufschein*, as its name at the top indicates. It is in the usual form and has religious precepts in verse form that are commonly found in these certificates. The following verses are transcribed for the purposes of record and study:

Taufschein by Johannes Renninger (1841)

1

Wann wir kaum geboren werden,
Ist vom ersten Lebens-tritt,
Bis zum kühlen Grab der Erden,
Nur ein kurzgemesz'ner Schritt.
Ach! mit jedem Augenblick
Gehet unsere Kraft zurück
Und wir sind mit jedem Jahre,
Allzureif zur Todtenbahre.

2

Und wer weisz, in welcher Stunde
Uns die lezte Stimme weckt,
Denn Gott hat's mit seinem Munde
Keinem Menschen noch entdeckt.
Wer sein Haus nun wohl bestellt,
Geht mit Freuden aus der Welt;
Da die Sicherheit hingegen,
Ewiges Sterben kann erregen.

3

Ich bin getauft, ich steh' im Bunde,
Durch meine Tauf, mit meinem Gott!
So sprech' ich stets mit frohem Munde,
In Kreutz, in Trübsal, Angst und Noth.
Ich bin getauft, des freu' ich mich,
Die Freude bleibt mir ewiglich.

4

Ich bin getauft, ob ich gleich sterbe,
Was schadet mir das kühle Grab?
Ich weisz mein Vaterland und Erbe,
Das ich bey Gott im Himmel hab'.
Nach meinem Tod ist mir bereit
Des Himmels Freud U[nd] Feyerkleid.

5

Ich bin getauft in deinem Namen,
Gott Vater, Sohn und heiliger Geist
Ich bin gezählt zu deinem Saamen,
Zum Volk, das Dir geheiligt heiszt.
O! welch ein Glück ward dadurch mein!
Herr, lasz mich deszen wurdig seyn!

The purport of the foregoing verses is that the path of life from birth to the coolness of the grave is but a short step and with each wink of the eye our strength wanes from year to year towards the bier of death. We know not in what hour we may hear the last call since God has not revealed it to any man. He who has set his house in order leaves this world with joy and those who do not invite eternal death. As I am baptized what matters the cool grave to me. I know my fatherland and inheritance that I have with God in heaven and that after my death there is prepared for me the garment of praise and the joy of heaven. I am baptized in the name of the Father, Son and Holy Spirit and I am numbered in the company of the redeemed.

The Baptismal certificates were large in size, usually 13 by 16 inches. The record was in the center and that afforded ample space for decoration. The decorations are of the widest range in design and color. All kinds of flowers are used, whose forms and colors mostly are such as to defy botanical identification. Birds of curious shapes and colors unknown in nature appear everywhere. Doves, parrots, cardinals, warblers, tanagers, eagles, and ever so many others with the gayest but unnatural plumage appear in the borders. We also find crocodiles, sheep, an occasional serpent, mermaid, angels and portraits.

Singularly the decorations are of the most joyful character—birds, flowers, leaping harts, children, angels with trumpets—while at the same time the text ever reminds the reader of the shortness of this life, of the approach of death, and the seriousness of this present, in view of his anticipated and probably sudden passing into eternity. Further considerations will be given to these decorations in the section on Symbolism.

Baptismal certificates were naturally greatly esteemed. They were framed and hung upon the walls of the home. Curiously enough many of them were buried at death with the persons baptized.

It became the practice for scribeners to prepare certificates with blanks and to peddle them from house to house. This is evident from the fact that frequent specimens are found with the same designs, decorations, colors and letter-forms but with the inserts in a different handwriting and with differently colored inks.

The illuminated *Trau-Schein* or Marriage certificate is comparatively scarce, although written and printed certificates are frequently found. Samuel W. Pennypacher in *Pennsylvania—the Keystone* (Philadelphia 1914) reproduces a manuscript which he labels as "a vorschrift marriage scene." Scripture texts are used but no family names appear. It was probably intended as a wedding gift.

An illuminated marriage certificate in my possession, with facts relating to birth and marriage in a rectangular central figure, surrounded with geometrical designs, flowers of various sorts, and scripture texts in hearts, all heightened with color, has the following:

> "Daniel Esch und Katharina Stutzmanin sind geheyrath im yahr Christi 1814 den 3 ten April und am selbigen tag copulirt und vollzogen worden. Gott gebe ihnen viel gluck und segen und gesundes, langes leben, in fried und ewigkeit."

The manuscript certifies to the birth of Katharina, November 25, 1793, in "Bruderswalley Township, Sommerset County."

Genealogical Records are generally to be found in the large family Bibles. They at times are beautifully engrossed and were done by professional penmen.

House Blessing
(*Haus Segen*)

THE *Haus Segen* is in substance a prayer to Almighty God for the preservation of the house from destruction through fire, storm or other calamity and for a benediction upon the owner, his wife and children, and upon all those who may go in and out. Frequently there are added prayers for a virtuous life and a happy entrance into Heaven.

"Der Segen Gottes Kron dies Haus" (The blessing of God crown this House) is the opening and characteristic prayer of the inscriptions, manuscripts and broad-sides generally referred to as Haus Segen. The origin and long continued use of these invocations rests in the attitude which the German had towards his home

To understand the sincerity of these prayers, consideration must be given to the physical energy required in the building of a house; to the importance of the place given to the home, and to family life; and to an ever-conscious religious faith which placed this present life under the cover of eternity.

The building of a house was a major undertaking in the life of the German Pioneer. In days when there was no power-driven machinery, the whole building process lay in arduous hand labor—in man-power. The stone was quarried, cut and conveyed by hand. The trees of the forest were felled with the swing of the axe. The lumber, when seasoned through the slow process of lapse of time, was squared with the adz. The physical labor involved was arduous and naturally led the builder into prayer to God for the preservation of that which literally was the work of his hands.

At this point I am faced with the temptation of using forbidden space for the description of a unique and intensely interesting manuscript associated with a Pennsylvania German custom. It bears the title of *Ein Zimmer-Spruch beym Auf-stecken des Strauszes.*

In other words it is an anthology of prayers and congratulations, and a program of rejoicing for a meeting of the builder, journeymen, owner and friends who have gathered at the completion of a building when a spray of flowers or branch of a tree is placed upon the completed building.

The manuscript is in the form of a booklet with a text of about twelve hundred words. It is written throughout in Gothic Fraktur letters; the title being in red and the text in black. An inscription on a fly-leaf bears the date of 1787. I hope an opportunity will hereafter be afforded to publish the entire manuscript. In connection with House-Blessings, it is pertinent to refer to two prayers which appear in the manuscript as a part of the ceremonies of rejoicing upon the successful completion of the building. The speaker presiding at the ceremonies says that the building was erected and completed through God's help and with his power and he, therefore, gives thanks to God that He permitted no one engaged in its construction to flinch or falter and that no disaster or other misfortune came to any and he prays that God may with His grace stand guard now and hereafter. Those who wish to make their own translation may do so by reading the original:

EIN ZIMMER-SPRUCH

beym Aufstecken des Strauszes

Diesen neuen bau haben wir aufgeschlagen; durch Gottes huelf und seine macht Haben wir diesen Bau zustand gebracht. Nun wollen wir dem lieben Gott dancken das er keinen hat lassen woncken, das keiner ist in ungluck kommen und sonst kein schaden hat genommen. Auch thun wir den lieben Gott bitten er wolle uns ferner in gnaden behüten.

Another prayer is offered for the preservation of the building and for the health and long life of its owner. In this prayer, God as the creator of the world and the upholder of everything created, is petitioned, through His grace, to preserve the building from hail and lightning, and from destruction by water or fire and to bless the owner, his wife, and children with health and long life.

> Herr Gott du schöpffer der gantzen welt der du durch deine macht alles erhaltst; Du wollst diesen bau erhalten, in gnad, vor hagel und grossem ungewitter das er dardurch nicht fall darnieder vor wasser und vor brand; darzu das gantze Vatterland, du wollest auch unserm bauherr geben ein gesundes und langes leben.

A purpose, deeper than a sense of duty, to build well and strong, lay in the heartfelt desire that the house should become the permanent seat of the home of his family—the Home-stead. Here dwelt not only his family, but his prayer was that it might also be the dwelling place of God. In his home, lay safety and contentment. Here was the very center of the life of the Pioneer. His deeply religious nature made him turn for a blessing to God, in whom his faith rested. His prayer was for a blessing upon his wife, his children and upon all who passed in and out. Not only were these the unexpressed prayers of his heart but the German builder gave outward expression of these prayers by cutting them into stone or carving them into wood and giving these cuttings and carvings a prominent place in his building.

The origin of these outward expressions of divine benediction, evidenced in House-Inscriptions, is found in the Fatherland of the German immigrant. As he built his house in the forests of Pennsylvania, his memory recalled the House-Inscriptions in wood and stone in the houses of his native land; and so he practiced, in a modified form, in the land of his adoption, the long established custom of his ancestors across the sea.

A House-Inscription, locally well known, is still to be seen in the house of Johannes Brunst, at Fegleysville, Montgomery County, Pennsylvania. The inscription, cut into a stone placed on the front of the house built in 1854, is as follows:

I

Hin geht die zeit
Her komt der Todt
O mensch thue recht
Und furchte Gott.

II

Das Haus ist mein
Und doch nicht mein
Es Kommt ein andere
Ist auch nicht sein.

I

Away passes time
Here comes death
O man, do right
And fear thou God.

II

This house is mine
And yet not mine
There comes another
And yet it is not his.

This is a beautiful illustration of the survival of a foreign custom; for these quatrains are to be found carved into wood and cut into stone in houses in Germany, Switzerland and Austria built centuries ago.

Those who desire to pursue this subject further are referred to two books:

Inscriptions from Swiss Chalets by Walter Lardner (Oxford 1913)
Hausspruche aus den Alpen by Ludwig von Hormann (Leipsic 1896)

These books are authority for the statement that the first quatrain on the Brunst house (hin geht die zeit) is well known in Switzerland and Austria. In virtually the same form, it appears on a house built in the early eighteenth century in Goldern, Switzerland.

The second quatrain (Des Haus ist mein) occurs in Switzerland and in the Tirolese section of Austria. It is also found in various localities in Germany and seems to be of ancient and general use among German builders.

Larden records the following parallel of the second Brunst quatrains upon a house in Switzerland (1890):

Dies Haus is mein
Und doch nicht mein
Der nach mir Komt
Dem wirds auch nicht sein
Ach, Gott, wer wird der letze sein.

In Pennsylvania, House Inscriptions in stone or wood are rare. Stones cut with the initials of the owner and of his wife, with a date, however, are very plentiful. These stones placed in gable ends or prominently in the front walls of the houses in the Pennsylvania German sections, are very well known. They are the evident remnants of the ancient custom relating to House Inscriptions.

The Pennsylvania German adopted the easier practice of putting his Haus Segen into manuscript or printed broadside and displaying it in a frame on the walls of his house. Haus Segens were printed in German at Ephrata, Reading, Allentown and Harrisburg, Pennsylvania. They were also printed at New Market, Virginia, and in other Pennsylvania German localities. These in a general way followed the old texts found across the sea, with additions and variations. It is not within the province of this monograph to deal with the printed broadsides. Reference will, however, be made to two for the purposes of the text.

John Bauman, Ephrata, Pennsylvania, printed Haus Segen broadsides at various dates. The following quotation is from a broadside (1801), printed within a heart in outline and a border of vines of leaves and flowers and with doves and parrots:

HAUS SEGEN

In Gottes namen geh ich aus,
Auch Herr regier du heut das haus;
Die Hausfrau und die kinder mein,
Lasz dir Gott befohlen seyn.
Bewahr mein herze, mund und hand;
Vor grossen lastern und vor schand.
Gib, das ich mein sach wohl richt aus,
Und wieder frolich komm zu haus. Dass
solches, O getreuer Herr, gereichen mocht
zu deiner ehr. Hut dich, fluch nicht in
meinem haus, oder geh bald zu thur hinaus:
Es mocht sonst Gott vom Himmelreich auch
strafen mich und dich zugleich.

The foregoing may be freely translated as follows:

In the name of God I go out
O God rule thou today this house.
To the housewife and children mine
Let God well pleasing be.
Preserve my heart, mouth and hand
from malicious slander and from shame.
Grant that I may my affairs do well
And happy again, to my house return;

So that the same may, O faithful Lord,
redound to thy honor.
Watch thyself; swear not in my house—
or soon through the door go out.
Otherwise God may from the Kingdom of
heaven punish me and you alike.

A manuscript in my possession, dated January 23, 1757, with text in fraktur lettering and a decorative border in dull colors, reads as follows:

1. Hit dich. Fluch nicht in meinem hausz. Oder geh bald zur thur hinaus es mocht sonst gott vom himmelreich straffen mich und dich zugleich.
2. Ich kam in ein frebdes land da stunt geschrieben an der wand bis fromm und sei verschwiegen was nicht dein ist das lasz liegen.
3. Wer in sein hertze sicht, der redt von keinem boses nicht Dann an ihm selbst jeder mann gebrechs genug werf mercten kan.
4. Red wenig und mach es wahr. Borg wenig und mach es klar. Lasz einen jeder wer er ist. So bleibt der auch wer du bist.

The admonition (Hit dich) against swearing in this manuscript and in the Ephrata, and in many printed broadsides, is recorded by Leonard as being carved in a Swiss house dated 1706 and occurs frequently.

The translation of the first paragraph appears above. The rest may be translated thus:

2. I came into a strange land. There stood written on the wall: Be pious and hold your peace. Leave that which is not thine where it is.
3. He that looks into his own heart, does not speak of his own badness. For in himself each man finds enough. . . .
4. Say little, and let it be true, borrow little and let it be clear, leave everyone where he is. That leaves you where you are.

HAUS SEGEN WITH NAME OF JOHANN FORRER

A manuscript, in fraktur lettering with birds in color, circa 1840, has among other things the following invitation to the visitor:

"Bleibb uber nacht in meinen hutten;
wascht eure fues an diesen ort; last
euch bis morgen fruh erbitten; dan ziehet
eure Strasse fort."

A free translation follows:

Stay over night in my dwelling,
Wash thy feet in this place.
Till morning seek what you will,
Then onward your journey pursue.

Another broadside is frequently met with. The central printed matter is surrounded with color work, featuring angels, birds, fruits etc. The following quotation (two out of four stanzas) is taken from a broadside printed by Johann Ritter and Company, Reading, Pennsylvania, although the same phraseology appears elsewhere:

HAUS SEGEN

I

Gott des Vaters Schopfers hand
Segne dieses haus und land
Dasz das futter und die Saaten
Immer mogen wohlgerathen
Das der viehstand wohl gedeyhe
Und sich senies segens freye
Das seine vaterliche gute

Haus und hof und stall und scheuer
Fur ungluck und besonders feuer
Immer quadlich behute.

II

Der Heil'ge Geist kehr hier auch ein
Und lasz es seine wohnung seyn
Heil'ge unser thun und laszen
Aus und eingang gleichermaszen
Heil'ge uns zum sel'gen sterben
Und mach uns zu Himmels-erben

The following free translation will give an inadequate idea of the foregoing:

HOUSE BLESSING

I

God the Father—Creator's hand
Bless this house and land.
That the fodder and the grain
Always may well produced be,
That the livestock may well increase,
And they his blessings freely have.
That his Fatherly kindliness,
House and yard and stable and barn,
From disaster and especially fire,
Always mercifully guard.

II

Let the Holy Spirit also herein move
And let it His dwelling be.
Sanctify our work and let
Out-and-in-going be alike
Sanctify us to a holy dying
And make us heirs of Heaven.

The prayer to protect the house from calamity, especially fire, may very readily be understood as being most sincerely uttered. Leonard records its appearance upon Swiss houses dated 1757, 1759, 1776 and quotes the following inscription upon a house with date of 1737:

Der hochste Gott disz haus bewahr
Vor wasser feuer und aller gefahr.

A free translation follows:

The highest God this house protect
From water, fire and all calamity.

The original manuscript of Haus Segen (Plate No. 36) has no date and there is no evidence as to the particular locality in which it was written and illuminated. Its probable date is 1815. The brownish letters have somewhat faded and because it may not readily be read in the reproduction, this beautiful blessing is now quoted:

HAUS SEGEN

Der Segen Gottes krön dies Haus
wo unsre Kinder gehn ein und aus.
Wir loben Gott dir danken wir
mit unsern Kindern für und für.
wo sie und wir gehn aus und ein
da lasz du uns gesegnet seyn.
Lasz unsre Lebenszeit und Jahr
zubringen christlich immerdar.
Gott Vater Sohn und heil'ger Geist
vom dem uns alle Gnad herfleuszt
gib dasz aus unsrer Kinder Mund
der Nam des Herrn stets werde kund.
Gib ihnen wahre Folgsamkeit

lasz ihre ganze lebenszeit
ein Abdrick deines Bildes seyn
und lehr sie stets das Böse sche'n.

It is difficult to follow all the words in the foregoing text, but the following in free translation is adequate as to substance:

May the blessing of God crown this house where our children go in
and out.
We praise God, Thee we praise,
We with our children for ever and ever.
When they and we go out and in, let
Thou us blessed be.
Let the time of our life and thereafter ever Christlike be.
God, Father, Son and Holy Spirit, from whom all our blessings flow,
Grant us that our children may have the speech to declare the name
of the Lord.
Let their obedience throughout their whole life be an imprint of thy
Image and teach them the evil to shun.

This manuscript is unusual in its decoration. The rose is most beautifully designed. The other flowers are conventionalized so that even the best informed botanist cannot identify it. The flowing border of unidentifiable flowers, in colors of brown and green—not true to nature—produce a most artistic effect. It would be difficult to find a bit of folk art more pleasing in design or color.

The more we study these Haus Segen manuscripts, the less we think of art and the more we think of their purpose. Their texts reveal an intense zeal for the establishing of a home in which there is purity and peace, and for the maintenance of a family of which God himself is a member.

In Plate No. 35 there is a sentiment of ancient usage:

Wer auf Gott vertraut,
Der hat wohl gebaut.

Leonard states that this is a quotation taken from a hymn written by Joh. Muhlmann (1573-1613). He found this inscription upon Swiss houses dated 1612 and 1744.

Freely translated, the following gives the substance but with regrettable loss of meter and rhyme.

Who in God has trusted
He has well constructed.

Verbal Labyrinths

1. Spiritual Labyrinth (*Geistlicher Irrgarten*)
   (The Fall and Redemption of Man)
2. The Seven Rules of Wisdom (*Die Sieben Regeln der Weisheit*)
   (Mystifying Arrangement of Words)
3. Spirals and Circles

THOSE who have visited Coney Island and other pleasure parks may have entered a mirror maze and wandered through its labyrinthine ways, where embarrassing situations were met in their effort to gain an exit. The two words *maze* and *labyrinth* suggest the idea of a complex path or route of some sort with winding and tortuous paths, which render it difficult for the person following it to find the way which leads to the exit or end.

The labyrinth has a fixed place in history. Herodotus about 450 B.C. describes it. It is a part of the early history of Egypt where it was used in the division of land, and in the layout of tombs and buildings. The readers of Hawthorne's *Tanglewood Tales* will recall the famous labyrinth of Crete, built by Daedalus and in which were annually imprisoned seven youths and seven maidens of Athens. In the center dwelt Minotaur, finally slain by Theseus who made his escape by means of a silk thread, one end of which was held by Ariadne, the beautiful daughter of King Minos. Designs in the form of the labyrinth are found on Grecian vases and in the layout of Roman pavements. During the Middle Ages the great Cathedral builders used it as a mural decoration and as designs for floor mosaics. At a later date the labyrinth was adopted in the layout of formal gardens in Italy, Germany, France, England and in the United States.

It is said that a labyrinth (Irrgarten) of a symbolical character occupied a large area in the garden of one of the Princes of Amhalt, a Duchy in Germany. It was allegorical in character and was intended to typify the course of human life. It was composed of streams and caverns with tortuous paths, covered in with hedges and trees. The visitor was met at every turn with some puzzling inscription or allegory and then he was again cheered on his way by flowers, by a sculptured object or by an assuring inscription leading him to the unseen but happy exit.

Those who are interested in the history of Mazes and Labyrinths should consult a book, with an exhaustive bibliography, by W. H. Matthews, entitled *Mazes and Labyrinths* (Longmans, Green & Co., London, 1922).

In Germany the spiritual labyrinth appears in print as early as 1630. In Pennsylvania, broadsides in German, entitled *Geistlicher Irrgarten,* were popular. I have seen the following imprints:

Heinrich Miller, Philadelphia 1762
Ephrata Brotherhood, Ephrata, Pa., 1788
E. Benner, Sumneytown, Pa. (about 1840)

Printer not named, Reading, Pa. (about 1830)
G. C. Peters, Harrisburg, Pa. (about 1830)

Our present interest lies in the fact that the Irrgarten was also produced by the Pennsylvania German penmen and illuminators. For the sake of clearness, however, a printed copy is here reproduced as being more readable than a manuscript (see Plate No. 37).

In a real labyrinth in a building or garden, the visitor physically travels through its devious ways. The broadside here reproduced is said to be a verbal labyrinth because the reader must keep turning and turning it so as to obtain a consecutive reading. The arrangement of the text is horizontal, first running from left to right, then again from right to left; vertical from top towards the bottom and then from the bottom towards the top. The reader does no traveling but he must make more than one hundred turnings of the printed page if he would read without a break and reach the end of the text which he will find at the place of beginning. Woe betide him if he errs in his turnings.

The broadside here reproduced as Plate No. 37 is entitled *Geistlicher Irrgarten* (Spiritual Garden or Labyrinth). The text is supported by Biblical Quotations referring to wandering sheep and states that in the spiritual garden-maze there are four wells of grace. (1) Man is first found in his happy state in Paradise with its four rivers, before the Fall. (2) A recital of the miseries with which man is beset by reason of the Fall. (3) Man's body returns to dust but his soul should engage in good works, faith and prayer to Christ so that rest may be found by the soul with God from whom it sprang. (4) How man yielded to Satan whereby his entire nature was destroyed and how he, like an erring angel, wandered away till God stretched out his arm of grace through his Holy Spirit and in Holy Scripture, as in a spiritual mirror, man beheld Jesus, saw and confessed his own miserable state, and sought to escape therefrom by calling upon God who through Holy Scripture showed him Christ and by faith in him he was directed to the true way of life and through which he reached happily everlasting righteousness.

I have a manuscript of this character, in color, and in which religious precepts are written on a running band which starts at one corner of the sheet and runs at right or acute angles in and out under and over through the other corners to the place of beginning.

DIE SIEBEN REGELN DER WEISHEIT
(*The Seven Rules of Wisdom*)

W. H. Matthews in *Mazes and Labyrinths*, above referred to, states that in the Latin Convent on the summit of Mount Carmel, Palestine, a visitor in 1876 found a "verbal labyrinth" displayed on a board hanging on the wall of an inner staircase. It was called "The Labyrinth of St. Bernard." It consisted of a number of words or phrases arranged in a square as follows:

LABYRINTHUS A DIVO BERNARDO COMPOSITUS QUO BENE VIVIT HOMO

DICERE	SCIS	DICIT	SCIT	AUDIT	NON	VULT
FACERE	POTES	FACIT	POTEST	INCURRIT	NON	CREDIT
CREDERE	AUDIS	CREDIT	AUDIT	CREDIT	NON	EST
DARE	HABES	DAT	HABET	MISERE QUAERIT	NON	HABET
JUDICARE	VIDES	JUDICAT	VIDET	CON-TEMNIT	NON	DEBET
NOLI	OMNIA QUAE	QUIA QUI	OMNIA QUAE	SAEPE	QUOD	

By selecting the words in the proper order five maxims are obtained by which man may live well. The first of these maxims, commencing with the word at the foot of the left-hand column, is *Noli dicere omnia quae scis quia qui dicit omnia quae scit saepe audit quod non vult.*

The remaining four injunctions may be read by similarly utilizing the words in the bottom row with those in the second, third, fourth, and fifth rows respectively.

Among the Pennsylvania Germans there were circulated manuscripts entitled "Die Sieben Regeln der Weisheit" (The Seven Rules of Wisdom). The arrangement of the words follows:

DIE SIEBEN REGELN DER WEISHEIT

THUE	NICHT	KANST	DEN	HOFFART
FRAGE		NICHTWEIST		FURWITZ
GLAUBE	ALLES	HOREST	ES	LEICHTSINNIGKEIT
GIB		HAST		VERSCHWENDUNG
SAGE	WAS	WEIST	IST	THORHEIT
URTHEILE		SIEHEST		FRECHHEIT
BEGEHRE	DU	MAGST	EIN	UNVERSTAND

The foregoing in translation is:

THE SEVEN RULES OF WISDOM

DO	NOT	CAN	FOR	PRIDE
ASK		DON'T KNOW		CURIOSITY
BELIEVE	EVERYTHING	HEAR	THAT	CREDULITY
GIVE		HAVE		PRODIGALITY
TELL	THAT	KNOW	IS	FOLLY
JUDGE		SEE		IMPUDENCE
DESIRE	YOU	LIKE	A	STUPIDITY

The foregoing verbal arrangement is read as follows:

DIE SIEBEN REGELN DER WEISHEIT

Thue nicht alles was du kanst den es ist ein Hoffart.
Frage nicht alles was du nichtweist den es ist ein Furwitz.
Glaube nicht alles was du horest den es ist ein Leichtsinnigkeit.
Gib nichts alles was du hast den es ist ein Verschwendung.
Sage nicht alles was du weist den es ist ein Thorheit.
Urtheile nicht alles was du siehest den es ist ein Frechheit.
Begehre nicht alles was du magst den es ist ein Unverstand.

THE SEVEN RULES OF WISDOM

Do not everything that you can for that is Pride.
Ask not everything that you don't know for that is curiosity.
Believe not everything that you hear for that is credulity.
Give not everything that you have for that is prodigality.
Tell not everything that you know for that is folly.
Judge not everything that you see for that is impudence.
Desire not everything that you like for that is stupidity.

Spiritual Wonder-Clock
(*Geistliche Uhrwerk*)

The Spiritual Wonder-Clock (*Geistliche Uhrwerk*) has analogous forms in the Christian Guide for the Hours (*Christlicher Stundenweiser*) and the Meditation for Twelve Hours (*Zwolf Stunden-Gedächtnisz*).

THE purpose of the Spiritual Wonder-Clock is the same as that of a Book of Hours, so well known in medieval days. The design takes various forms. In one of these there is a grandfather's clock and to each hour on the dial there is attached a circle containing a spiritual admonition. In others the meditations are enclosed in twelve hearts surrounding a large central heart. The following is an abridgment of twelve precepts in as many hearts arranged around a large heart which has a House Blessing.

1. One supreme need of the soul is to seek Jesus.
2. Two ways of life are set before us; shun the broad and seek the narrow.
3. Three persons in God the Bible teaches. Praise Father, Son and Holy Spirit.
4. Four ends of life face the soul, Death, judgment, hell, heaven. Seek that which leads to peace.
5. Five wounds in the crucified Christ who calls all to him for rest.
6. Six days for the creation of a world of beauty by God who only can renew and refine the heart.
7. Seven words spoken by the Lamb on the Cross. Take them as the spirit of life.
8. Eight persons were saved in the Ark from the flood. May Christ Jesus be an ark to me.
9. Nine cured lepers did not return thanks but only the tenth. Think of what God has done for you.
10. Ten commandments are set before my eyes. Let my spirit heed them with Jesus as my guide.
11. Eleven out of twelve were true. May Jesus help me to remain faithful to the end.
12. Twelve pearly gates there are in Zion City. May the soul never tire till it attain salvation to enter therein.

Book-Plates
(*Bucherzeichen*)

THE word *Bucherzeichen* is not found in the dictionaries of the dialect spoken by the Pennsylvania Germans. Its use in Germany, however, is well known. Its English equivalent is Book-plate or Ex-libris.

The ponderous *Oxford Dictionary* defines a Book-plate to be "a label, usually pasted inside the front cover of a book, bearing the name or crest of the owner, or other device, indicating ownership, etc."

W. G. Bowdoin in *The Rise of the Book-plate* (New York 1901) points out that "the mission of a book-plate always was and always will be to indicate the ownership of the books in which they find a place."

W. J. Hardy, a noted specialist on this subject, in his work on *Book Plates* (London 1893), states that the term Book-plate is applied to "marks of ownership pasted into books." As to their origin, he says that a variety of opinions exist as to "whether, in the first instance, the use of Book-plates was suggested by a desire to commemorate a gift or as a mark of ownership."

> "Some of the earliest mechanically produced book-plates are certainly commemorative of gifts; but I think we must accept as book-plates, to all intents and purposes, the six fourteenth century examples mentioned by Herr Warnecke in his *Die Deutschen Bücherzeichen*, an excellent work on German book-plates. These are heraldic *drawings* on the parchment leaves of Italian manuscripts, which also bear an inscription of possession by the particular individuals whose arms are represented."

The authorities concede to Germany her claim of introducing the indication of book-ownership by means of Book-plates. It is interesting to refer to the first two printed Book-plates. The plate of Jean Knapensberg about 1450 is still extant. About 1480, a Book-plate, or "gift-plate" was inserted in a book given by Hildebrande Brandenburg of Biberach to the Carthusian monastery of Buchsheim.

In view of this German centuries-old custom, it is not surprising that, although in a modified form, the Pennsylvania Germans continued this beautiful practice of putting into their books, evidences of gift or of ownership, artistically designed and brightened with color. The reader is now asked to turn to Plates Nos. 30, 31, 32, 33. Pennsylvania German Book-plates are found in hymnals, Bibles, catechisms, musical notebooks, and schoolbooks in print and manuscript. These Book-plates were made in great numbers, although I have found no reference to them in any book dealing with Book-plates.

In the books are many marks of ownership. On the fly leaves frequently appear family names, religious texts and admonitions to a higher life. Many of them have Book-plates with faultless calligraphy and artistic decorations and illuminated with brilliant colors. In the Book-plates herein reproduced the text is in Gothic lettering and German script. The flowers used in the decorations are beyond botanical identification, although in one of the plates the rose has evidently been suggested by the name Rosina. The birds, arrayed in gay colors, are beyond recognition. An indication of the general character of the book is followed with the owner's name. Charles Dexter Allen, in his *American Book-Plates*, makes no reference to these plates and his extensive bibliography includes American, English and French books and references only. Just why he omitted a German Bibliography is not apparent. If the reader is interested, he will find an extensive German Bibliography in *German Book-Plates* by Karl Emich Count zu Leiningen-Westerburg (London, Bell & Son, 1901).

Pennsylvania German Book-Plates were made in great numbers. In a modified form, engrossed and heightened with brilliant colors, they are found in manuscript schoolbooks. The Pennsylvania German was devoted to singing. Manuscript books with musical notes were beautifully written and frequently their title pages were artistically designed with the owner's name and with decorations in color.

The specimens here reproduced are true Book-plates. About forty books with these inserts are before me for study. They invariably are of the size of the page of the book. They have, however, a stub about an inch wide which has been folded over and used for pasting the plate into the book. In them we find, of course, the thing which, at once, stamps them as Book-plates, the names of the owners. Frequently, the date of the birth of the owner is given and occasionally the sign of the Zodiac is noted. At times the name of the donor also appears. Then, too, there are quotations from the Bible, or moral precepts pointing to a good life. As in other Book-plates, compliments are at times paid to the non-returning borrower of the book.

Among inscriptions of interest may be noted the following in free translation:

1. Time passes every day
   Who knows how near the end may be.

2. Guide me, dear Savior mine,
   And lead me into the Kingdom thine.

3. This book to me is precious.
   Who takes it is a thief;
   Who returns it is a Child of God.

4. This book is presented to the owner
   for instruction to the Glory of God.

5. Write my name in the Book of Life.

6. To do the will of God is to do well.
   He does best who does with a willing heart.

I have in my collection a book in manuscript entitled *A Collection of Musick Adapted for the Harpsichord.* On the front cover there is a drawing or design of an oval surrounded by an irregular scroll, on one side of which there is an inscription the letters of which are in reverse order so that it may be properly read when held in front of a mirror. The inscription is as follows:

"M. Hillegass Junior, His Book July 1747."

There is also a printed label indicating the ownership of Michael Hillegas and dated 1747. The book of music is interesting as containing examples of songs, marches, minuets, gavots, jigs, sonatas, etc. There is also an extensive section for the clarinetto.

AN ENGRAVER OF BOOK-PLATES

It is appropriate that we should step aside for a moment from our main subject to call attention to an eminent Pennsylvania German, David McNeely Stauffer. He was born in Lancaster County, and he became an engineer of distinction. In 1907 the Grolier Club of New York published his well-known book entitled *American Engravings Upon Copper and Steel.*

Stauffer was an amateur designer of Book-plates and there are approximately fifty to his credit. They are armorial in character and are drawn with strict regard to the rules of heraldry.

He designed a Book-plate for the late William U. Hensel, one of the Presidents of the Pennsylvania German Society. The plate shows the arms of the ancestor family of Hentzel. It also depicts the interior of a wood-carver's shop. Among the other plates engraved is that of George Steinman, of Lancaster, Pa., in which is shown a coppersmith in his shop and a street scene in Old Lancaster.

Among other plates designed by Stauffer is that which was done for the Donegal Chapter of Lancaster County, Pa., of the Daughters of the American Revolution, and also that of Chauncey M. Depew.

Book-Mark

(*Lese-Zeichen*)

A BOOK-MARK (*lese-zeichen*) is used by the reader to mark the progress of his reading or to indicate the place of a particular passage in the text.

Count zu Leiningen-Westerburg in *German Book-plates* (Dennis translation) says that the word *Bucherzeichen* (book plate) must be distinguished from *Buchzeichen* (book-mark).

The originals, reproduced in Plates Nos. 8 and 29, are glibly said to be Book-Marks; the only authority for the statement being the fact that they were found in books. That apparent fact may be mere coincidence. Moreover these color designs are frequently found in company with other bits of personal property, which would hardly be classed as Book-Marks. I have frequently found in Bibles, Hymnals, Catechisms and other religious books the articles following: writings in fraktur, color designs, Bible texts, dried flowers including petals of the rose, saffron and Johnny-jump-up; fronds of ferns, leaves of trees and shrubs, locks of hair, bits of colored paper, pieces of calico and other textiles, manufacturers' labels, cures for diseases, recipes for soap, money (not much or often), paper cut work, rewards of merit, funeral notices, chromos, and many other articles "too numerous to mention."

One question: Are these Book-Marks?

My general answer is that these bits were preserved because they had an aesthetic, religious, informational or sentimental value to the owner and surely there was no better depository for their safekeeping than the Holy Bible and kindred books.

True Book-Marks were, however, frequently found. They consisted of pieces of linen thread and pieces of paper extending above the top margin of the book. The ever-present dog's ear was perhaps the Book-Mark most frequently used, to the terrible disgust of the lover of books as books.

The Texts

A STUDY of the text in the Manuscripts is tedious because it is partly in Gothic Fraktur letters and, what is more difficult, partly in script. The handwriting of no two manuscripts is the same. The substance of the text relates to religious and moral teaching. There are quotations of Bible texts, hymns, songs, moral precepts, proverbs and admonitions to a better life. The Hymns quoted show denominational connections. The hymns and songs are not only such as were brought from the Fatherland but many were composed on American soil. Rules of conduct are given by schoolmasters for their scholars. It is not proposed to make detailed translations but outstanding texts will be considered for their substance.

A SONG OF SUMMER

The manuscript reproduced as Plate No. 23 was done by Susanna Heebner in Montgomery County, Pennsylvania in 1807. I have called it "A Song of Summer." It is a song written by Paulus Gerhardt (1607-76) and it is still being sung by children in Germany. How interesting it is to find this early German poem in Pennsylvania in 1807. The poem as found in the *Oxford Book of German Verse* is as follows:

Der Sommerzeit

by Paulus Gerhardt

(1607-76)

Geh aus, mein Herz, und suche Freud'
In dieser lieben Sommerzeit
An deines Gottes Gaben;
Schau an der schönen Gärten Zier
Und siehe, wie sie mir und dir
Sich ausgeschmucket haben.

Die Bäume stehen voller Laub,
Das Erdreich decket seinen Staub
Mit einem grünen Kleide;
Narzissus und die Tulipan,
Die ziehen sich viel schöner an
Als Salomonis Seide.

Die Lerche schwingt sich in die Luft,
Das Täublein fliegt aus seiner Kluft
Und macht sich in die Wälder;
Die hochbegabte Nachtigall
Ergötzt und füllt mit ihrem Schall
Berg, Hügel, Tal und Felder.

Die Glucke führt ihr Völklein aus,
Der Storch baut und bewohnt sein Haus,
Das Schwälblein speist die Jungen.
Der schnelle Hirsch, das leichte Reh
Ist froh und kommt aus seiner Höh'
Ins tiefe Gras gesprungen.

Die unverdroszne Bienenschar
Fliegt hin und her, sucht hier und dar
Ihr' edle Honigspeise;
Des süszen Weinstocks starker Saft
Bringt täglich neue Stärk und Kraft
In seinem schwachen Reise.

Ich selber kann und mag nicht ruhn:
Des groszen Gottes Groszes Tun
Erweckt mir alle Sinnen;
Ich singe mit, wenn alles singt,
Und lasse, was dem Höchsten klingt,
Aus meinem Herzen rinnen.

Ach, denk' ich, bist Du hier so schön,
Und läszt Du's uns so lieblich gehn
Auf dieser armen Erden,
Was will doch wohl nach dieser Welt
Dort in dem reichen Himmelszelt
Und güldnem Schlosse werden?

Welch hohe Lust, welch heller Schein
Wird wohl in Christi Garten sein?
Wie musz es da wohl klingen,
Da so viel tausend Seraphim
Mit eingestimmten Mund' und Stimm'
Ihr Allelujah singen?

THE INSTRUCTION OF YOUTH

The manuscript reproduced as Plate No. 21 was, doubtless, done by the pious school-master, Christopher Dock, and its text aptly begins with these words: *Gott fuerchten, lieben, ehren, soll man mit ernst die kinder lehren.* The following is a free translation of the text:

God to fear and love and honor
Should man with earnestness to children teach.
He who in the favor of God would live
Must such teaching not resist.
Through the fear of God man avoids the sin
For through sin man earns the curse.
A child that keeps God before his eyes
In this amazingly wicked world
And to God also in humility prays
That he will his soul well attend
Such child that keeps God in view
Will his holy angels watch.
He that God fears not will godless live—
Wild become and finally wholly godless be—
Such godless child will to torment go,
To pangs of hell and to suffering come.
Therefore while still in the time of grace
So let us ready and prepared be,
Even as lambs to hear the voice of Jesus,
Our hearts to open and to follow Him
Who will guide us into that fold
Where the holy lambkins are.

CHANTICLEER

Chanticleer's call in rhyme was known to all Pennsylvania German children. It appears in manuscripts and in many A B C Books, or Primers—often on the cover. The substance of the rhymes is that chanticleer crows his loud "kückrikü," or call, to waken the children early so that they may learn that there is gold in the mouth of the morning hours—and further to permit chanticleer to wake them early and willingly; that they clothe, wash and comb themselves, then pray and hasten to school and learn to know self and God so that they may be prepared for death.

For record purposes, it is appropriate to give the German text of Chanticleer:

Der Hahn

Der hahn kraht laut sein Kückrikü!
Die Kinder aufzuwecken früh,
Zu lernen in der morgenstund:
Den morgenstund hat gold in mund

Lasz, mein kind, den hahnen dich
Früh aufwecken, williglich.
Kleid dich, wasch dich, Kamm dich, bet,
Und alsdann zur schul hintret,
Lern erkennen dich und Gott,
Willst du seyn geschickt zum tod.

IN PRAISE OF VIRTUE

In Plate No. 26 we find a beautiful description of *Virtue*. Freely, a portion of the text runs as follows: Virtue is the ornament of youth and age. Treasure and crown without virtue will fall and die like Absalom. Virtue as the best portion is an aid to eternity. It brings fortune and prosperity on earth. The world, pleasure, honor, fortune will perish. To live a rich and noble life and to join the hosts angelic after death, walk in the path of Christ; be content and virtuous in heart and mind as was the Lamb of God and search and follow the word of God.

CHRIST ON THE CROSS—A MEDITATION

Plate No. 20 shows a manuscript, dated 1771, which has for its text a hymn which is printed in the 1803 Edition of the Mennonite Hymnal. It portrays Christ crucified for sin alone and teaches salvation through his sacrifice.

A VISION OF HEAVEN

In Plate No. 22 the text presents a vision of heaven where angels evermore give praise.

PRAISE TO GOD

Heaven and earth and air and sea and every created thing join in praise of their Creator. See Plate No. 17.

CONFIRMATION

Plate No. 17 contains admonitions for a religious life so as to live eternally with God, the Father, and was evidently presented upon confirmation.

Quotations from other manuscripts appear in other sections of this monograph at their appropriate places. The texts which have been given are sufficient to give a fair idea of their substance. A complete study would require a separate monograph.

Designs

OUR consideration thus far has been based upon the various uses and purposes for which manuscripts were made. Let us now study them from the standpoint of design. The names of these manuscripts have been determined by their various purposes. It is desirable that there should be a generic term applying to them as a class. The term *Fraktur-Schrift* is already in use although its derivation has not been generally understood. It is not surprising to find peculiar and often inadequate words adopted by English writers in books and magazines, and in catalogs issued by antique dealers and auctioneers. The following terms have been used: Pen-paintings, birth, marriage and baptismal certificates, prayers, illuminated writings, book-marks, school-exercises, American primitive, Tauf-scheins, Fractur, picture by a Pennsylvania Dutch artist, school-master's paintings; and Pennsylvania Dutch fractur. These and similar terms have appeared in auction catalogs issued by American Art Association, and Ritter-Hopson Galleries; in "Practical Book of American Antiques" by Eberlin and McClure and by Henry C. Mercer in his brochure herein referred to; and in papers appearing in various magazines.

This begins our inquiry into the derivation and meaning of the word *Fraktur*. By way of beginning, let me say that the German word *Fraktur* (fractur) refers to a certain design of Gothic letters.

In Lambert's *Pennsylvania German Dialect Dictionary* we find the following:

Fraktura; Gothic letters or figures. (G. Frakturen)

Frakture; G'frakturt, to write in Gothic characters. Verb formed from fraktura.

Muhlenberg and Schipper's *German-English Worterbuch* (1812) gives the following definition:

Fractur: fractured, Gothic letters, characters.

In Daniel Berkley Updike's *Printing Types, their History, Forms and Use* (Cambridge Harvard University Press 1922) we find:

"The first type cutters and type founders were merely servile imitators of the manuscript letter-forms to which they were already accustomed. We can understand little about the design of our present printing types, if we are not familiar with the characters in the black-letter and Humanistic manuscripts which just preceded, or were contemporary with, the invention of printing. There appears to have been no thought in the minds of the early printers other than to reproduce manuscripts quickly and inexpensively; and although many early printed books were very beautiful, both in type and arrangement, because modelled on fine manuscripts, I doubt if fifteenth century printers so consciously intended to make their books beautiful as is commonly supposed. What an early printer was intent upon doing was to produce a printed book which resembled manuscript as closely as possible; and that such a man failed to recognize any great divergence in theory between a book in manuscript and a printed volume is shown by his obvious endeavor to follow in type the written letter of the manuscript. . . . So it is clear that we can have no knowledge of the types of to-day and their history without knowing the history of types back to the invention of printing and that we can have no knowledge of the first types or their relative place in the schemes of things unless we know calligraphers formed the letters in their manuscript book-hands. Nor can we tell how the letter-forms themselves came to be unless we know the history of the alphabet, of the various forms of Latin writing, and its vicissitudes in different countries up to the invention of printing. The next step in the study of type is to learn and recognize the various forms or 'tribes' of type and the subtle differentiations between varieties of the same general form of type face. . . . One type form used in the fifteenth century is

Gothic by which the medieval text or black letter is always meant. In the fifteenth century German Gothic or black-letter fonts, a differentiation of type-faces began to show itself in the last twenty years of the century, between types that were somewhat pointed and a rounder, more cursive Gothic letter. . . . The first type was called *Fraktur*. The second ultimately became known as *Schwabacher*."

Updike's work contains typical facsimile reproductions of specimen printing showing the several forms of type.

Theodore Low DeVinne in *Plain Printing Types* (The Practice of Typography Series, New York 1900) says:

"The able printers of classic texts at Strassburg and in other cities, supported as they were by authority of Albrecht Dürer, could not induce German readers to accept the Roman character. They preferred pointed letters. . . . The Bible-text of Gutenberg, which is the basis of modern black-letter; the profusely ornamented and flourished letters of the 'Theuerdanck' which is the model of modern *German-text*; the round-Gothic, or semi-Gothic of Schoeffer, a hybrid of Roman and black-letter; the Schwabacher and the fractur—all these had their admirers. The *fractur* was at last accepted as the standard form of text-type."

DeVinne, however, makes the following comment:

"The *Roman face* is almost always in most request, for Roman is the character preferred as a text-letter by all English-speaking peoples and all the Latin races. Its only serious rival in general literature is the fraktur, or the popular face of German type; but even in Germany, Roman is largely used as the text-letter for scientific books."

For our purposes it is necessary to go somewhat further into the origin of the Fraktur letter-designs. Richard W. Ellis, a typographer of distinction, kindly handed me a brochure entitled, *Leonhard Wagner der Schopfer der Fraktur* (ein beitrag zur geschichte der deutschen Schrift) by Konrad F. Bauer (Frankfurt am Main 1936).

The author shows Leonhard Wagner to have been the creative designer of the Fraktur type (Gothic with sharp points or spikes) and that he was employed by King Maximilian. Wagner was a Benedictine Monk attached to a cloister in Augsberg and produced in 1507 a manuscript of one hundred letters, no two of which are alike in design. Wagner's "Schreib-buch" is still in existence and bears the title:

"Proba centum scripturarum diversarum una manu exaratarum fratris Leonhardi Wagner: Hundert Schriften von ainer hand der kaine ist wie die ander."

Plate No. 38 is a reproduction of one page of Wagner's manuscript of letters. Not only does it give the clearest idea of what Fraktur lettering is but it also presents the general form in which the Pennsylvania German Vorschriften are designed, as a comparison with Plate Nos. 3 to 7 will show.

The original application of the word Fraktur as a letter-form was gradually enlarged to include the decorative features in design and color which were added to beautify the lettering. The term Fraktur-Schrift gradually came to be applied to all manuscripts of this class, even when they were without any lettering whatever. Thus the term *Fraktur-Schrift* may well be accepted as the proper generic term.

LETTERS

This brings us to a study of Pennsylvania German designs of letters. At Ephrata, Pennsylvania, there was a writing-school before 1750 for the Brothers and Sisters in the Cloisters of the Seventh-Day Baptists. They were seriously engaged in designing letters. I have the glass negatives of one of their manuscript books of letters. There are two sets of the capitals, one of which has ornamental borders with free-hand designs, with flowers, birds and vines. Some of them are of singular design and proportion. For the most part, however, the capitals as a whole seem to me to be too broad and overloaded.

Pen-work requiring great skill was done at Nazareth Hall, a Moravian School, at Nazareth, Pennsylvania, before 1800. Some one should give it publicity.

THE LETTER B

As has been stated, the highest artistic skill was devoted to the design and treatment of initial letters in Medieval Manuscripts. William Morris, in *Some Notes on the Illuminated Books of the Middle Ages*, says:

> "The great initial B (beatus vir qui non) of these books (The Psalters) affords an opportunity to the illuminator, seldom missed, of putting forth to the full his powers of design and color."

Plate No. 18 is the reproduction of the letter B in a Pennsylvania German Manuscript. It is undated and unsigned. It was evidently done by a member of the Heebner Family in Montgomery County, Pennsylvania. My opinion is that it was illuminated by Susanna Heebner about 1810. Its beauty of design and delicate coloring entitle it to be placed in the company of the ancient manuscripts.

The featuring of the initial letter in manuscripts, of the vorschrift class, is generally carried through the first line across the top of the page. This is in some form of the fraktur type and the remainder of the text usually appears in script. It has always seemed to me that the addition of script to fraktur lettering lessens the artistic effect of the general layout. Very few of the manuscripts show letters and numerals in script of calligraphic value.

DESIGNS IN GENERAL

The Birth and Baptismal certificates have the greatest variety of decorative designs. On the average they are 13 inches by 16 inches in size. The factual statement occupies the small space in the middle of the sheet and it leaves large margins for the free play of the designer. Of course, the other manuscripts of various sorts have no limitation as to space or fashions to be followed. They are left to the freedom of the artist. Let us in this section briefly catalog the various designs which were used and in the sections on Symbolism and Text they will enter into the running text.

Living in the open country, it is to be expected that designs would be suggested by things seen in nature round about and we find the following:

Sun	Pink (Negle)
Moon	Rose
Stars	Lily
Rainbow	Violet
Dove	Apple
Parrot	Vines
Eagle	Leaves
Peacock	Trees
Chanticleer	Butterfly
Scarlet tanager	Fruit
Yellow Warbler	Pomegranate (perhaps)
Lamb	Grapes
Horse	Corn in Ear
Tulip	Children

There was very little attempt at portraiture of persons. In some manuscripts, however, there are Portraits of individuals such as Washington and Andrew Jackson. In a few wedding certificates, there are pictures of a bride and groom, which may have been an effort at portraiture.

Religious symbolism and some mythological hang-overs, as we shall see, had their part and so we find:

Angels	The New Jerusalem
Cross	Flames of Hell
Crown	The Devil
Arrow	Pelican
Pilgrim with Staff	Mermaid
Heart	Crocodile
The Crucifixion	Dragon

There was a general adaptation of geometrical designs and they appear in the use of the following:

Circles	Spirals
Triangles	Columns and Arches
Squares	Interlacing designs

Buildings and articles of household furniture and adornment produce pictorial effects of:

Dwelling houses	Vases
Castles	Tables
Candles	Ark

Forms are used for decoration and not for scientific delineation. There is a large variety of plants, flowers and birds which cannot be scientifically identified, resulting in a large class of nondescripts.

GENERAL PRINCIPLES

A general survey of hundreds of Pennsylvania German Manuscripts reveals certain general features. No landscape effects are attempted to any extent. The rules of perspective drawing are absent. Generally speaking, also, the use of plants, flowers, birds and animals appear as separate settings without being incorporated into the decorative whole. To this there is a notable exception in Plate No. 21. The dove or peacock is, in an ingenious and most effective manner, woven into the letter D.

The proper study of symbolism in the designs in Pennsylvania German Manuscripts makes it necessary to call attention to the fact that the general character of the designs in the manuscripts on the one hand, and on pottery, barns and furniture on the other hand, greatly differ. There is somewhat of uniformity of motif in each class, and peculiar to itself. In pottery, furniture and barn paintings, there appears the professional element which is absent in the manuscripts, excepting possibly the Baptismal certificates and in Bible Family records. Esther Stevens Fraser in the *Pennsylvania Bulletin* for November, 1925, in an article on "Pennsylvania German Painted Chests," says:

> "The fact that a number of chests showing identical workmanship in painted decoration exist is of great importance. It proves the incorrectness of the general supposition that these dower chests were painted at home by amateurs who felt the urge to decorate. It supports the belief that they were ornamented by professional furniture painters who traveled from farm to farm wherever work was in demand, just as the traveling cobblers and traveling tinsmiths did in the same sparsely settled locality."

The element of production by the professional also appears in the decoration of pottery and the painting of designs on barns.

"TOO NUMEROUS TO MENTION"

Children who have to live in an apartment or in a house with a flat roof are being deprived of a chief joy. Every person who, in childhood, resided in a house with a sloping roof will thank architect and builder for its construction. An attic is the storehouse of a fastidious housekeeper. The more important fact is that it is the cherished treasury of childhood memories. The contents of the attic are the things which will some day be described in an auctioneer's sale-bill as "articles too numerous to mention." I have often wondered why there is so much poetry in things that are useless.

Thus far a classification of Fraktur-Schriften into major classes has been attempted. In my Portfolios there remain scores of manuscripts "too numerous to mention" and defying classification. These will now be referred to in a very general way.

Frequently met with are the *Music-books* with notes. They seem to have been made for the particular scholar whose name very likely appears in a title page, with elaborate designs and color schemes, in which are used flowers, vines, angel-faces with wings, and free-hand drawings. The Ephrata books of music, with notes, are marvels of quill-penmanship and the spaces at the end of the musical scores are often filled in with exquisite designs in lace-work. (See Plate No. 28.)

In early days printed text-books were unknown. It was a splendid contribution to mental development that the scholars had to make their own *Text-Books* under the direction of the school-master. Many of these were beautifully written and the title and the chapter and section headings often were done in color. Some one should make a comprehensive study of the Text-Books compiled in the schools of the Pennsylvania Germans.

Christmas cards or greetings do not turn up in these manuscripts. *New Year's greetings* were exchanged. In Plate No. 19 such greeting is beautifully engrossed but the joy of the greeting is made somewhat somber by reminding the recipient of the flight of time and the advisability of preparation for eternity.

Pictorial Drawings were also attempted. I have specimens of a man astride a running pig; of a boy on a hobby horse; of an archer; of a man with a gun shooting at a deer; of a groom handing to his bride a cup, the contents of which are not made known.

Reference has already been made to *Portraiture* and in addition to those already mentioned is the face of the Duchess of Brunswick which is to be found in certain Baptismal Certificates. I have an Ephrata manuscript with a Pilgrim—probably a portrait of Conrad Beisel.

Hearts were used in plentiful abundance. They appear in simple outline form enclosing a verbal text; in a solid color of brilliant red, and in one specimen a scarlet heart pierced with an arrow is in a Baptismal Certificate,

Among the unusual attempts at beautification is *punch work* and *cut work*. There is before me a large Baptismal Certificate (dated 1818 in Lancaster County, Pennsylvania) beautifully designed with four birds actually incorporated into a running border. The colors are red and blue and the portions of the design which are cut out demanded great skill. In some instances designs were punched with a needle giving an appearance similar to punched brass-work.

There is a large residue of individual nondescript sketches defying nomenclature. In this class are birds, flowers, trees, vines, leaves, animals, houses, castles, Noah's arks, scripture texts, letters of the alphabet, acrostics, points of the compass, numerals, free-hand designs of all sorts and specimens showing the use of color.

Implements and Materials

PICTURES of the tools or implements used by the German Illuminators are depicted in the title page of Bolt's *Illuminir Buch* reproduced in Plate No. 1. The reader may name them for himself. The tools depicted in this title page are discussed by Daniel V. Thompson, Jr., in his translation of Cennino Cennini's *Il Libro dell'Arte* on page 20 (Yale University Press, 1933).

QUILL-PEN

The pen is the first tool or implement we think of. That took the form of a quill, for so-called steel pens were not manufactured for general use until about 1830.

The *A B C Buch*, printed at New Market, Virginia (1817-1820), states that the second, third and fourth quill of the left wing (the fowl is not named) is preferred. These are prepared by putting them into boiling alum-water and letting them remain for fifteen or twenty minutes. The outer skin having been removed, the quill is then dried by putting it in hot sand or in an oven or by holding it over a fire.

KNIFE

The same *A B C Buch* states that the knife for cutting the pen-point should have a small sharp-pointed blade. It should be sharpened by using a piece of calf-leather fastened to a piece of wood, first putting cotton between the leather and the wood.

Just how the cutting was done does not appear. It evidently had to be learned by actual practice. My father, who died in 1908, always preferred to write with a quill-pen. Sometimes he cut them with a pen-knife. He also used a little tool or device made in England and which I still have. It is probably seventy-five years old. The quill, partially cut, was placed into a little tube and by pressing a lever on which there was the die of a pen-point, the cutting was virtually completed and ready for writing.

PENCIL

I have a number of partially completed manuscripts. Some of them are preliminary sketches with ink, and others with lead of some sort. Just what material was used for that purpose I do not know.

INK-WELL

On the authority of the Shenandoah County, Virginia, *A B C Buch* an ink-well of glass is the best (glaserne dintenfass). One of the most interesting wells, sometimes found in antique shops, is pneumatic with a nozzle that has its opening into the barrel at its base. The one in my collection is made of glass, deep blue in color. It was presented to me and used fifty-five years ago when I was a scholar in the small stone school-house which then stood near Bally in Berks County, Pennsylvania. The school-house was located in a typical Pennsylvania German Community, as is shown by the Family names of some of the scholars in attendance: Bauer, Bechtel, Borneman, Diehl, Ehst, Eschbach, Fuchs, Heydt, Koch, Moyer and Stauffer. The school was in charge of Morris Y. Schultz to whom, as my first teacher, I pay a much deserved tribute of appreciation and affection. His ancestors belonged to the Schwenkfeldian group who arrived in 1734. He was tall and slender, with black hair and a sallow complexion; sympathetic in approach and leading his pupils with a kind and assuring manner. He spared the rod and, I fear, spoiled, at least, some of his children.

BRUSHES

The application of pigments in solutions, more or less heavy, required the use of a brush. An examination of Plate No. 13 shows brush-work in the margin. The translators of *De Arte Illuminandi* (Yale University Press 1933) point out that the distinction between pen-work and brush-work is an important one. In medieval days inks or liquids, with white of egg or glair, were applied with pens, but the tempering of pigments with gums brought the brush into use.

Just what animals supplied the hair for the brushes is not recorded. Free and easygoing writers are always ready to tell us how the brushes were made but my researches have not revealed any evidence which I would care to use as the basis of a statement, even for a guess.

RULERS

Rulers were used to lay out the designs. It may be supposed that any straight-edge would suffice and I was surprised to add to my collection a ruler with decorative carvings. It is triangular in form and twenty-four inches long. It has mountings of pewter, each of its three sides being less than an inch wide. One side has carvings of small rectangles and triangles, running vines and tulips. Another side has carvings of the letters of the alphabet and the date 1769. On the third side are carved letters arranged in groups with intervening stars as follows:

E * LI * SA * BETH * NO * TI * GERM * DA * N * BACH

To me those letters spell the names of two persons romantically linked together: Elisabeth Notiger and M. Danbach.

COLOR BOX

Boxes were made for the pigments and bottles for inks. In my boyhood days, I had a series of small bottles for inks of various colors—some of which I compounded myself with more or less success—usually less. In Henry C. Mercer's *Survival of Illuminative Writing Among the Pennsylvania Germans* there appears a cut of a "Paint Box" which is said to be in the possession of the Bucks County Historical Society, Doylestown, Pennsylvania. It is about a foot long, six inches wide and has several compartments for bottles, quill-pens, brushes, and dry colors.

PAPER

The study of the paper used in the production of these manuscripts is most interesting. The quality ranges from the finest handmade rag-paper to the poorest grades. In days when paper was largely obtained from local paper-mills, and in not very large quantities at that, the pen-man used whatever grade was available. Frequently there are water-marks which have rich historical value. They furnish credible evidence as to locality and date with the necessary caution that there be a check and double-check in these days of reproducing antiques and the offering of them as originals.

In Colonial days, deeds for the conveyance of real estate were often written on parchment. I have seen no specimens of parchment used for illumination in color. In passing, let me note that forms of deeds were printed on parchment at the Ephrata Press about 1765.

COLORS

How did they make their colors? What chemicals did they use to prevent fading? How did they produce that glossy or varnished effect? Where did they get their color recipes? Why are some of the colors crackled or crazed? These and many similar questions were repeatedly asked by those to whom I submitted Pennsylvania German Illuminated Manuscripts for examination.

The quest for satisfactory answers followed long and uncharted ways, particularly difficult at times, because I am not an artist, neither do I have a knowledge of the chemistry of inks and pigments. The answers which are reasonably satisfactory to myself are here set forth in outline and will serve as guides for those who desire to make definitive studies.

I like to think of color as an attribute of light, and that the purpose of its creation was to set up a thing of beauty for the pleasure of man. Factual-headed scientists will doubtless disagree with these somewhat poetical views and declare, on the one hand, that color is not an attribute of light, but rather an interpretation and report given by the brain of the fact of the contact of light with that marvelous organ of the human body—the eye. On the other hand, the scientist will also likely discard the fanciful view of creative purpose which I have expressed and he will perhaps suggest that the reason why man enjoys color lies in the fact that for countless years he has been subjected to it and he gradually fell into the way of liking it; so that he now derives pleasure therefrom, etc., etc.

A sunset is not painted with pigments and it leaves no trace of its existence when it fades. An artist, however, uses solid or liquid substances to produce his color effects. The colors appearing in these manuscripts are produced by the use of inks and pigments. Column-writers have suggested that their methods of producing colors were primitive and the results crude. An examination of hundreds of manuscripts has led me to the conclusion that these colorists were not mere experimenters in the making of inks and pigments. They used recipes which were handed down not only by tradition but in many cases in manuscript and print. The German has always required the free use of color to satisfy his aesthetic taste. The processes of making inks and pigments by the Germans are centuries old. This will be substantiated by a reference to four books printed in Germany and in Pennsylvania.

It is noteworthy to observe that the first systematic work for the use of painters is a manuscript written by Theophilus, a German Monk of Paderborn (Westphalia), Germany. It was written in the twelfth century and bears the title: *Diversarum Artium Schedula by Theophilus called also Rugerus*. This treatise is said to be at least one hundred years earlier than the famous *Libro dell'Arte* by Cennino d'Andrea Cennini. Theophilus went back to Byzantine sources and his work contains recipes similar to those found in contemporary painters' manuals of the southern countries. For the purposes of this monograph an interesting observation may be made. Casual writers, when referring to Pennsylvania German colors, have lightly thrown out the idea that, because of the lack of adequate artists' materials, they used such simple things as the gum of the cherry tree and the white of eggs. Theophilus gave a recipe for tempera, a subject which will be presently referred to, and he used cherry gum as a vehicle and light colors were applied with the watery residue of beaten white of egg. Somehow, the recipes of Theophilus used in the twelfth century have been transmitted to the Pennsylvania Germans in the nineteenth—a span of seven hundred years.

With the invention of printing, the art of producing illuminated manuscripts gradually became less and less. The Germans, however, continued the color decoration of manuscripts and of the printed page for several centuries thereafter. In corroboration of this statement, attention is directed to three German Craftsmen's books dealing with the art of illumination (*Illuminir-Bücher*). These three manuals, which are in my possession, are of great rarity, because they had no literary merit and were easily spoiled by the craftsmen who used them. They were published before the English Manual imprinted at London in 1573, entitled *A very proper treatise wherein is briefly set forth the art of Limning*.

The first one is Boltzen's *Illumnirbuch* (1566); the second is a *Kunstbüchlin* of 1566; and the third a *Kunstbüchlin* of 1560. The titles of these Manuals are as follows:

1. *Illuminirbuch,* Künstlich alle Farben zumachen und bereyten, Allen Schreibern, Brieffmalern, und andern solcher Künsten Newen zugesetzten Kunstücklin, vormals im Truck nie auszgangen.
Durch Valentin Boltzen von Rufach n.p. 1566.

(*Freely translated*)

1. Illumination Book: How artistically to compound and prepare all colors. Pleasant and useful to know for all writers, letter painters and all those who love this kind of art; completed by some recently added methods about which nothing was printed before. By Valentin Boltzen in Rufach 1566.

2. *Kunstbüchlin* auff mancherley weiss Dinten und aller handt Farben zu beriettten. Auch Goldt und Silber sampt allen Metalen auss der Federn zu schreiben. Mit viel anderen nützlichen Künstlin, Schreibfedern und Pergamen mit allerley Ferben zu ferben. Auch wie man Schrifft und gemälde auff Stähelene Eisene Waffen bund der gleichen Etzen soll. Frankfort, 1560.

(*Freely translated*)

2. Art booklet: How to prepare inks and all sorts of colors in different ways. Also gold and silver and all other metals, to be used for writing. With many other useful recipes, to dye quill and parchment with different colors. Will be pleasant and useful to know for all writers, letter painters and those who love this kind of art. Frankfort, 1560.

3. *Kunstbüchlin* grundtlichen rechten gebrauchs aller kunstbaren wercklent. . . . Jede farben zubereyten, erhalten, bessern und widerbringen. Als zum malen, schreiben illuminiren, vergulden, etc. Franckfort, 1566.

(*Freely translated*)

3. Art Booklet: For thorough and right use by all craftsmen. About brass work, done in or without fire, for Alchemistic and natural reason, namely: to harden, soften, melt, refine, separate, test, solder, etch, form, cast, etc. To prepare, preserve, improve and reproduce each color, in order to paint, write, illuminate, gild and engrave, etc. Frankfort, 1566.

Boltzen's *Illuminirbuch* was first published at Basel in 1548. The 1566 edition in my possession has 120 pages of text and a complete index. Scores of recipes are given for all sorts of colors and liquids used in the tempera methods of painting. Here the colorist will learn how to make inks of all colors and pigments for red, violet, brown, yellow, green, blue, black and white. The *Kunstbüchlin* of 1560 and the *Kunstbüchlin* of 1566 also contain a large number of similar recipes.

We now jump into Pennsylvania and find a German book printed in Allentown, Pennsylvania, in 1819, which bears the following title:

Oeconomisches Haus und Kunst-Buch oder Sammlung ausgesuchter vorschriften zum nutzen und gebrauch für land und hauswirthe, handwerker, kunstler und kunst-liebhaber Zusammengetrogen aus den besten Englischen und Deutschen schriften von Johann Krauss, Allentown, Gedruckt bey Henrich Ebner, 1819.

The original text of this book has been ascribed to Christian Fischer of Wurtemberg (1811).

Krauss' book contains recipes for household and art use. For our purposes there are recipes for black, green, blue and red inks; for red, blue, green and other pigments; and for liquids used in the tempera method of painting. A careful study of these recipes used by the Pennsylvania Germans in 1819 shows that many have the essential ingredients appearing in Boltzen's *Illuminirbuch* in 1566.

In addition to the foregoing manuals dealing with colors, I direct the readers' attention to the following pertinent publications:

1. *De Arte Illuminandi* (The technique of manuscript illumination) a Twelfth Century Latin Manuscript translated by Daniel Varney Thompson, Jr., and George Heard Hamilton (Yale University Press 1933).
2. *Egg Tempera Painting* by Vaclar Vytlacil and Rupert D. Turnbull (Oxford University Press 1935).
3. *The Materials of The Painters Craft* by A. P. Laurie (T. N. Foule's of London 1910).
4. *The Materials of the Artist and their Use in Painting* by Max Dorner (Harcourt, Brace & Co. of New York 1934).

A study of the foregoing publications will lay the ground-work for anyone who wishes to understand the fundamentals of inks and pigments, color materials and the various methods of their application. With these principles in mind, it is safe to say that one of the methods used by the Pennsylvania Germans was painting in tempera. This is shown by the recipes appearing in Krauss' book and also by the appearance of the colors themselves. And what is meant by tempera? Without using quotation marks, let me use as the most easily understood answer thereto portions of the text appearing in the eleventh edition of the *Encyclopaedia Britannica* (Vol. xx, p. 490, Vol. xxvi, p. 578):

> *Tempera* (the Italian term) or Distemper, is a method of painting in which solid pigments are employed, mixed with a water medium in which some kind of gum or gelatinous substance is dissolved to prevent the colors from scaling off. . . . Various media have been used for tempera work, such as the glutinous sap of the fig and other trees, various gums which are soluble in water, and size made by boiling down fish-bones, parchment and animals' hoofs. A mixture of egg and vinegar has also been found to be a good medium, especially when it is desirable to apply the colors in considerable body or impasto.
>
> *Tempera Painting:* The binding substances used in the tempera processes may be classed as follows: (1) Size preferably that made from boiling down cuttings of parchment. Fish glue, gum, especially gum trajacanth and gum arabic (the Senegal gum of commerce); glycerin, honey, milk, wine, beer, etc.
>
> (2) Eggs in the form of (a) the yolk alone; (b) the white alone; (c) the whole contents of the egg beaten up; (d) the same with the addition of the milk or sap of young shoots of the fig tree (which was used in the south of Europe); (e) the contents of the egg with the addition of about the same quantity of vinegar which was used north of the Alps.
>
> (3) Emulsions in which wax or oil is mingled with substances which bring about the possibility of diluting the mixture with water. Thus oil can be made to unite mechanically (not chemically) with water by the interposition either of gum or the yolk of egg.
>
> Of these materials it may be noted that a size or gum tempera is always soluble in water and is moreover always of a rather thin consistency. The latter applies also to white of egg. On the other hand the yolk of an egg makes a medium of greater body, and modern artists, especially in Germany, have painted in it in full impasto. The yolk of egg or the whole egg slightly beaten up may be used to temper powdered pigments without any dilution by means of water and the stiffest body can in this way be obtained. . . . The yolk of egg is really itself an emulsion as it contains about 30% of oil or fatty matter though in its fluid state it combines readily with water. Egg yolk must be regarded as essentially an oil medium. As it dries the oil hardens and ultimately becomes a substance not unlike leather that is quite impervious to water. Hence while size tempera when dry yields to water, egg tempera will resist it. . . . Theophilus prescribes a tempera of gum from the cherry tree and with some pigments white of egg.

Let the foregoing quotations from the *Encyclopaedia Britannica* be summed up briefly: In painting in tempera the pigments are "tempered," or mixed with some liquid or medium to bind their separate particles to each other and to the surface to which they are applied.

The color-work appearing in the Pennsylvania German Illuminated Manuscripts is produced with the use of inks, water colors, and water colors in tempera. Of inks nothing will be said here. I wonder, however, how many readers (all of whom know how to use ink) are able to describe adequately the nature of ink and how it differs from other color materials? The ordinary water color is said to be "transparent" and it appears dull and without any gloss.

The gloss or shiny appearance is produced by using water colors in tempera. All of the foregoing methods were used in the Pennsylvania German Illuminated Manuscripts.

The use of colors varies in the manuscripts produced by varying religious, community or other groups. The colors used by the Brothers and Sisters in the Cloister at Ephrata in Lancaster County, Pennsylvania, were subdued in tone. An examination of more than fifteen musical notebooks in the Historical Society of Pennsylvania, the State Library at Harrisburg, Pennsylvania, in the Congressional Library and in my own collection, shows illuminations in light brown, light blue, pale green, lemon and dull red tints. In many pages the chemicals of the black inks have eaten their way clear through the paper. In other instances the black has faded into a brown, giving a sepia effect to the whole. The colors have a wash effect such as would be produced by applying ink with a brush. Transparent watercolors, without tempera, were evidently used. Brilliant colors were not used. An Ephrata Manuscript before me depicts a pilgrim on a journey surrounded with spiritual texts. Black ink, now turned into brown, has been used throughout and the only color is a mere bit of red on the wing of a bird in a tree. That is characteristic of the Ephrata manuscripts. Brilliancy of color is avoided. Plate No. 28 is characteristic.

Among the Schwenkfelder group in Montgomery County, Pennsylvania, the opposite use is made of color-tints. In the manuscripts produced by them are to be found a great variety of colors, brilliantly treated and glossy in appearance, as will be seen by turning to Plate No. 23 and Plate No. 26.

Among the Mennonites the manuscripts inspired by Christopher Dock were mostly of the transparent water-color type without tempera. In their hymnals, bibles, catechisms and other religious books, however, are to be found Book-plates of great beauty with brilliant and glossy colors in tempera.

Baptismal certificates appeared in great numbers and their production became commercial. In many instances the designs were crude and the colors carelessly dashed upon the paper. In them, however, the student will find the greatest variety of inks, pigments, tints, washes, brush effects, and other elements which will aid him in arriving at their nature and methods employed.

Let it be recalled that yellow, red and blue are the primary colors which form the basis for all other colors, and that the color reproductions herein are the result of four printings, yellow, red, blue and black. Those who produced the Pennsylvania German Manuscripts had recipes for all these and they knew how to use them.

Daniel V. Thompson, Jr., in *The Materials of Medieval Painting* (Yale University Press 1936) says:

> "The glossiness of rubrics was an important consideration in medieval books; and the chief instrument controlling it was the modification of the glair-binder by the addition of yolk of egg."

In *"Die Land und Haus-Apotheke"* by Johann George Homan (Reading, Pa., 1818) there are recipes for black, blue, green and red inks and colors. The recipes leave a lot of guesswork as to what quantities are to be used in compounding but the valuable thing about them is that they show the use of vinegar, egg, honey—ingredients used in tempera work.

Johann Krauss in his *Haus und Kunst-Buch* (Allentown, Pa., 1819) gives directions for the preparation of Temperatur-wasser zur malerey mit Wasserfarben (the liquid for water-color painting in tempera). After having given a translation of Recipe No. 250, reference will then be made to recipes in Boltzen's *Illuminirbuch* (1566).

Krauss' recipe is as follows:

Temperatur-Water for Painting with Water-Colors
(Krauss Recipe No. 250)

For fixing water-colors take gum Arabic in order to hold the particles of the dye together, because it easily dissolves in water. But it has the disadvantage that, if entirely dried out, it becomes brittle, breaks easily and together with the dye it cracks off the base. It is necessary therefore to try to correct this disadvantage by other admixtures. The best way is to add gum of Senegal, which always contains some humidity, to make it soft and tough. Cane sugar and sugar candy also moderate the strong drying out and contracting of the gum, and besides make the dye easy to be handled with the brush. . . . Therefore take ¾ ounce of gum Arabic and ¼ ounce of gum of Senegal, pulverize both, enclose it in linen, leaving room enough to be able to flatten it with the hand. Put this bag in a quart of water, leave it in there, stir it once in a while, and within 24 hours the gums will have dissolved so that you can take the bag out. Then add ½ ounce of pulverized sugar candy and keep it for use in a corked up glass. After having cleaned the dyes with water mix them with a small portion of gum water and stir this up. With a little brush spread a specimen of it on your nail and try, by passing your thumb over it, whether after being dry it will stay or be wiped off. In the latter case add more gum water, but be careful and do not add more than absolutely necessary, because an excess of gum deprives the color of its substantiality and makes it slimy.

Valentin Boltzen in the *Illuminirbuch* (1566) gives at least eight recipes for the making of "temperatur wasser." Without copying any of them, it is most informing to point out that in his recipes we find the use of gum arabic, gum tragacanth, egg, rock-candy. The old recipes used in Germany naturally followed her sons across the sea. It would be surprising if they had not been used by the Pennsylvania Germans. These ancient receipts did not represent primitive experiments and were well seasoned indeed.

Daniel Thompson in *The Materials of Medieval Painting* (Yale University Press 1936) says (p. 57):

> "Just what gum arabic is, even nowadays, is something of a question and what it was in the Middle Ages is still more uncertain. For our purposes it does not particularly matter what kind of acacia yielded it, whether it was what we call *Acacia Arabica* yielded it or what we call *Acacia Senegal*, or some other, quite possibly some variety now extinct. It is quite clear that some gums that were not "arabic" at all passed under its name in medieval Europe. It is hard for us to realize how very superficial the identification of raw materials used to be. If the gum of a cherry-tree or a plum tree looked enough like gum arabic, gum arabic it became in medieval trade. Cherry-trees and plum-trees and almond trees all yielded gums which were used in place of gum arabic and along with it, though their solutions are quite different from solutions of gum arabic. . . . We should not allow ourselves to feel too superior to the Middle Ages about this business of nomenclature for there is a good deal of so-called gum arabic in trade to-day that has never seen an acacia bush, but is made from dextrin in imitation of the natural product."

The following recipes for inks and colors are to be found in Krauss' *Haus und Kunst-Buch* and the *Illuminirbuch* by Boltzen has scores of similar recipes without repeating them here. The following recipes are also given to show how the inks and colors used by the Pennsylvania Germans were compounded.

Carmine

Take one ounce of the most beautiful carmine and let it boil in a porcelain pot with ¼ pint of distilled water for 4-5 minutes, then gradually add one eighth of 1/4 pint of ammonia and stir it with a clean wooden stick. This causes an effervescing, and therefore, if you want avoid its flowing over, you have to take a pot of double size. After all the ammonia is added let the whole thing boil for two more minutes. Then let it cool off and keep it in the same pot for 24 hours. Hereafter pour the fluid off the sediments into a clean glass. The fluid will be of an even more beautiful color than the carmine and is perfect for use. As above, let the sediment boil with the same quantity of water and ammonia and the result will be the same. Only nature may produce as beautiful a rose-color as this will be.

Brownish-Red

Red-wood, alum and gum arabic are essential ingredients. The method of compounding has interesting features which will not be here detailed.

Violet

Log-wood (blau-holz), common alum mixed as above. Different shades may be obtained by mixing with brownish-red.

Lemon

Kreuzbeeren, common alum, gum arabic are the principal ingredients.

Gold Yellow

Annotto, potash, gum arabic are used.

Blue

Berlin blue, hydrochloric acid, and gum tragacanth are mixed as above.

Green

Verdigris, weinstein (tartar) mixed as above and different shades are obtained by mixing with it lemon or blue.

In *Das Grosze A B C Buch* by Ambrosius Henkel (New Market, Shenandoah County, Virginia), are recipes for Inks as follows:

About the Black Ink

Take 8 ounces of pounded gall nuts, 4 ounces of fine rasped logwood, boil both in 6 quarts of water until about half of it will have boiled down, then strain it through a piece of flannel; add 4 ounces of Copperas, 3 ounces of gum Arabic, one ounce of Blue Vitriol, and one ounce of sugar candy to the strained broth, mingle until everything will be melted, keep it in a well corked up glass jar for use.

About the Red Ink

Take three pints of good vinegar, 4 ounces of fine rasped Brasilian wood, boil it slowly in a tin or earthen vessel, on a coal fire for about half an hour. Then add 4 ounces of alum and one ounce of pulverized gum arabic; as soon as everything will be melted, strain through a strainer. Keep it for use in a well corked up bottle.

About the Green Ink

Take 1/4 ounce of verdigris, and 1/8 ounce of Cremor Tartari and 1/2 ounce of water, mix it well in a glass.

About the Yellow Ink

Take 1/4 ounce of Gum Guti Gambog, mix it with one ounce of water; if it becomes too thick, take more water.

About the Blue Ink

Grate indigo with honey and the white of an egg, each as you please; thin it with water until it will be liquid. Or take indigo and grate it with gum water. Depending on whether you want the ink dark or light, you can take more or less water.

History

IN A previous section it was pointed out that the art of illumination as practiced by the Pennsylvania Germans was a survival of the art of the Middle Ages. To that must be added the statement that it also was a Revival of the art which flourished in undulating waves for a period of one hundred years, roughly speaking between 1745 and 1845. It appears in Pennsylvania and other States wherever Pennsylvania Germans lived. Let us briefly review this Revival.

EPHRATA, PENNSYLVANIA

The first distinctive Revival appears in the Cloisters of the Brotherhood at Ephrata in Lancaster County, Pennsylvania, about 1745. Ability to produce Fraktur-Schriften was regarded as a spiritual grace. The designing of letters of the Fraktur type was highly developed, as has been seen in the section on Designs.

The decorative features reached their height in two Music Books produced by the Brothers and Sisters for Conrad Beissel about 1750. With the death of Conrad Beissel in 1759 the work of the Brotherhood declined rapidly and virtually ceased upon the death of his successor, Peter Miller, in 1789. Throughout the entire period music books with notes were produced with distinctive penmanship and decorations in color. See Plate No. 28.

So far as my studies have gone, I am of the opinion that the Ephrata Revival had no appreciable influence upon other Pennsylvania German groups.

In *Chronicon Ephratense* (Translated by J. Max Hark, Lancaster, Pa., 1889) we find:

> "They (the choral-songs) were brought to light, partly printed, partly written, Anno 1754, under the title: 'Paradisiacal Wonder Music,' which in these latter times and days became prominent in the occidental parts of the world as a prevision of the New World, consisting of an entirely new and uncommon manner of singing, arranged in accord with the angelic and heavenly choirs. Herein the song of Moses and the Lamb, also the Song of Solomon, and other witnesses out of the Bible and from other saints, are brought into sweet harmony. Everything arranged with much labor and great trouble, after the manner of singing of the angelic choirs, by a Peaceful one, who desires no other name or title in this world."
>
> "Some time during the night was fixed for the school-hour, and two Brethren were appointed teachers; but they showed such diligence in the school during winter that they neglected their domestic duties, which rendered it necessary to close the school. But the Superintendent, in consideration of the fact that such gray heads had paid so much honor to the work of God, in so far that they suffered themselves to be children again, had a music book for four voices written for them, which he presented to their Community. Their veneration for this music was so great that everyone wished to possess the book, and whoever had it accordingly fell under judgment, as happened yonder with the ark of the covenant. The book thus wandered from house to house, till at last nobody wished to have anything to do with it.
>
> "After the Superintendent had accomplished such an important work for the benefit of the spiritual Order in Ephrata, it was resolved, at a general council, that both convents present him with a worthy reward as a testimonial of filial esteem. This was to consist of two complete music books, furnished for all voices, one of which was to be made by the society of the Brethren, the other by that of the Sisters. Both parties put their most skillful members to the task. On the part of the Brethren three of them worked at it for three-quarters of a year. It contained about 500 tunes for five voices; everything was artistically ornamented with the pen, and every leaf had its own

head-piece. The Superintendent's name stood in front, skillfully designed in Gothic text; around it was a text of blessing added by each Brother. The work of the Sisters was not less remarkable. It was artless and simple, but something wonderful shone forth from it, for which no name can be found.

"These two books were reverently presented to him, and the Brother deputed thereto thanked him in the name of the whole Brotherhood for his faithfulness and care. He accepted their present graciously, and promised to remember them in his prayers. There were some instances when the Superintendent showed himself to be a great man, and this was one of them. Many might object that he was ambitious, but those who knew him more intimately, know how far he was from it. But the fact is, he was to make manifest the manners of the New World among his followers, and how everyone must esteem his neighbor higher than himself; and herein did his disciples faithfully follow him, according to the simplicity of those times.

"Before we conclude this chapter, let us mention the writing-school, where the writing in ornamental Gothic text was done, and which was chiefly instituted for the benefit of those who had no musical talents. The outlines of the letters he himself designed, but the shading of them was left to the scholar, in order to exercise himself in it. But none was permitted to borrow a design anywhere, for he said: 'We dare not borrow from each other, because the power to produce rests within everybody.' Many Solitary spent days and years in these schools, which also served them as a means of sanctification to crucify their flesh. The writings were hung up in the chapels as ornaments, or distributed to admirers."

CHRISTOPHER DOCK AND HIS SCHOLARS

The educational work of Christopher Dock at or near Skippack, in Montgomery County, Pennsylvania, has already been considered. Fraktur-Schriften entered largely into his methods of teaching. Not only did he use these manuscripts as rewards for good work but his scholars were taught the art of penmanship with decorative features. Dock died in 1771 and many of his scholars continued the practice of the art for years to come. Dock's influence marked a definite Revival in Montgomery County during a period of approximately forty years, from 1760 to 1800. See Plate No. 21.

THE SCHWENKFELDER GROUP

The Ship St. Andrew landed in the Port of Philadelphia the Schwenkfelder group, who settled in Montgomery County, Pennsylvania. They and their descendants for a century after were remarkable penmen. The forms of lettering appearing in the voluminous books in manuscript have a style of their own. In their decorative work they used colors of the greatest variety and brilliancy.

The work of many calligraphers of Heebner, Krauss, Kriebel and other Schwenkfelder families are to be found to this day. The high water mark of the Schwenkfelder Revival is the work of Susanna Heebner about 1807. See Plate No. 23 and Plate No. 26.

FOLK ART

The Revival of the art became general among the Pennsylvania Germans, being more marked in some communities than others and changing with the years. As has been said, we may look for these manuscripts for a period of one hundred years, from 1745 to 1845, approximately. The period of the highest and most general development may be said to extend from 1800 to 1835. During that period the Pennsylvania Germans attained one of the objects of art which William Morris in his "Notes and Fears for Art" (London 1901) stated to be:

> "Art made by the people and for the people as a joy to the maker and the user."

The rapid decline of the practice of the art began with the introduction of the public school system in Pennsylvania and it is generally said to be due to that fact. There is, however, another and a deeper reason and that lies in changing fashions. Customs, habits and practices vary with the likes and dislikes of the people. That was probably true in this case and the public schools afforded other outlets for self-expression.

PENMEN AND COLORISTS

Nothing will better illustrate the statement that here we have the practice of real folk art than to give the names of those who did this work. Here follows a list of 107 men and women whose manuscripts have survived. Among them is only one, Christopher Dock, whose name appears in the Dictionary of American Biography. There were, of course, many others. This list represents only those which I have seen.

Name	Year
Abraham Anders	1784
Anna Anders	1793
George Anders	1779
Joseph Anders	1805
Johannes Bar	1765
Andreas Bauer	1795
Andreas B. Bauer	1833
Abraham Bechtel	1838
Gerhard Bechtel	1810
Isaac Berret	1822
Jacob S. Bicksler	1829
David Bixler	1843
Martin Breehall	1813
David Buckwalter	1869
Johann Bussmann	1810
Christian Cassel	1772
Huppert Cassel	1769
Johannes Clemens	1816
John N. Detweiler	
Martin Detweiler	1788
Abraham Dirdorf	1781
Christopher Dock	1765
Joseph Egolf	1765
Mahlon Erb	1844
Philip Geisinger	1791
Henry N. Gerhard	1856
Rebecca Gerhard	1858
Harry Gise	1846
Jacob Gottschall	1800
Isaac Gross	
Jacob Gross	
Abraham Hackman	1786
Abraham W. Heebner	1832
Anna Heebner	1831
Heinrich Heebner	1842
Isaac Heebner	1767
Susanna Heebner	1807
Abraham Hess	1795
Jacob Hill	1797
Jacob Hillegas	1811
Elizabeth Hoffman	1793
Maria Hofern	1796
Abraham Huber	1790
Johannes Huber	1808
Sara Jackels	1788
Ferdinand Klenk	1875
Johannes Klinger	1814
Aaron B. Kriebel	1875
George Krauss	1866
John Krauss	1828
Susanna Kraus	1865
Abraham Kriebel	1782
Andrew Kriebel	1835
Anna Kriebel	1854
Catharina Kriebel	1840
David Kriebel	1763
David Kriebel	1805
Deborah Kriebel	1843
Elizabeth Kriebel	1809
Joseph Kriebel	1813
Maria Kriebel	1804
Rosina Kriebel	1816
Susanna Kriebel	1804
Margaretta Krumm	1818
Abraham Landes	1765
Agnes Landes	1783
Heinrich Landis	1786
Rudolph Landis	1814
Elizabeth Moyer	1813
Martin Moyer	1835
Abraham Oberholtzer	1829
John Heinrich Otto	1772
Jacob Overholt	
Sarah Reinwald	1847
Johann Jacob Sasserman	1758
Jacob Sautter	1762
Christian Schneider	1784
Johannes Schulof	1762
Benjamin Schultz	1781
Christopher Schultz	1826
George Schultz	1781
Isaac Schultz	1791
Johannes Schultz	1817
Jonas Schultz	1846
Jonas Y. Schultz	1848
Lea Schultz	1843
Lydia Schultz	1832
Samuel Schultz	1833
Sarah Schultz	1846
Solomon Schultz	1836
Susanna Schultz	1852
William Schultz	1821
Johannes Schumann	1821
Jacob Johannes Schweisfort	1809
Jonas Seibert	1844
Abraham Seybert	1812
Samuel Siegfried	1810
Christian Stauffer	1769
Johannes Stauffer	1817
John Stover	1852
Christian Strenge	1803

Elizabeth Weber	1843	Abraham Yeakel	1780
Henry Weiss	1791	Christopher Yeakel	1772
Maria Wiegner	1772		
Samuel Wissler	1806		

AN ITINERANT PENMAN

There came a day when the commercial penman arose. In my collection there is the working note-book of Ferdinand Klenk, who lived in Jackson Township, Lebanon County, Pennsylvania. He was an itinerant penman, traveling from house to house in the rural sections and entered in the family Bible the record of birth, marriage and death. The note-book is dated January 1, 1875. In it are samples of hand-writing with the prices which he charged for his work. The cost of writing, rather engrossing, one name with the date of birth is ten cents; with the addition of the place of birth fifteen cents; with the addition of the parents' names twenty-five cents; etc. In a letter from Millcreek Township, Lebanon County, Pennsylvania, to his wife, December 25, 1875, beautifully engrossed, he states that Christmas Day finds him in the western end of Lebanon County, traveling with horse and buggy. He has a large amount of work recording the births of children and the writing of baptismal certificates (Viele Geschaffte mit Kinder underschreiben und Taufschein machen). He states that he can't work fast enough to suit his customers and complaints are made because he did not call sooner. He is receiving a welcome everywhere.

Here then we have a splendid example of Folk Art—Practiced by the people; taught to the children in the schools; covering a large geographical area, and extending over a century of time. Truly this Revival of the art of illumination met the requirements of the splendid definition of Folk Art laid down by Horace Cahill in *American Folk Art (The Art of the Common Man)* (The Museum of Modern Art 1932) when he says:

> "Folk Art is the expression of the common people, made by them and intended for their use and enjoyment. It is not the expression of professional artists made for a small cultured class and it has little to do with the fashionable art of the period. It does not come out of an academic tradition passed on by schools but out of craft tradition plus the personal quality of the rare craftsman who is an artist."

Symbolism

IT IS astonishing how great a portion of our speech, both spoken and written, is given over to figurative language. The most effective method of driving home a thought by speaker and writer is through the use of simile, metaphor, allegory, parable, fable and emblem. In the Gospel according to St. Mark, Christ's method of teaching is recorded thus: "Without a parable spake he not unto them." In like manner artists draw pictures of things, not simply to produce a pictorial likeness, such as is shown in a photograph. Their aim is to add an element which will through association or analogy typify or suggest some fact, idea or truth. The artist's picture of something is the symbol of something else. The language of reproduction is direct and factual. The speech of a symbol is indirect and suggestive.

It is the easiest thing in the world for the individual with a lively imagination to indulge in dreams of symbolism when he looks at a century-old manuscript. The creator of the design has gone to his long home and the interpreter knows that no reply can come from him. Thousands of sermons are based upon texts that are mere statements of fact but are used by way of metaphor, simile, or type to support the structure or theme of the sermon. Such use of a text may be effective but it is not an application of its original mission.

". . . Learned commentators view
In Homer more than Homer knew."

It is the purpose of this monograph to deal with folk-art and not to consider the religious or philosophical faiths or beliefs of particular persons and their methods of teaching, symbolical or otherwise. Among those so excluded, by way of illustration, are Johannes Kelpius and Conrad Beissel.

Kelpius is generally thought of as the leader of the so-called "Pietists" who came into Pennsylvania at a very early date. In *The German Pietists of Provincial Pennsylvania* (Philadelphia 1895), Julius F. Sachse undertakes to establish that they were followers of the Rosicrucian teaching and he illustrates his book with hundreds of the emblems and symbols of that cult. The illustrations, however, are not reproduced from manuscripts written in Pennsylvania but are taken from foreign sources. The teaching of Kelpius was through hymnody and dissertation and was not graphically presented. In my examination of Pennsylvania German Illuminated Manuscripts I have kept in mind the Rosicrucian emblems reproduced by Sachse and also such as are to be found in Rosicrucian Treatises and Charts. I have failed to find in these manuscripts such emblems or symbols as would warrant the conclusion that Rosicrucian principles were a part of Pennsylvania German faith and practice.

Students of this subject must consult *Secret Symbols of the Rosicrucians of the 16th and 17th Centuries* (Aries Press Chicago 1935). The Symbols are reproduced in color and the text is an English translation of the *"Geheimne figuren der Rosenkreuzer aus dem 16ten und 17ten jahr hunderd"* (Altona, Germany 1788).

Conrad Beissel was the organizer of the Cloister life at Ephrata, Pennsylvania. In *The German Sectarians of Pennsylvania* (Philadelphia 1899) Julius F. Sachse refers to Beissel as "the Rosicrucian recluse of the wilds of the Conestoga." That is a picturesque but very inadequate statement. Fundamentally Beissel's faith and practice rested in the principle of absolute subjection to God and his unrestrained response thereto. In a manuscript of 150 pages, written by Peter Miller to Benjamin Franklin, and now in my possession, Miller says that Beissel regarded himself as standing under some invisible authority which did actuate him; that he was never governed by his own advices but stood in subjection to God; and that in all his actions he was under some supernatural power to which he was bound to conform and that he must not quench the spirit.

As is well known, Beissel expressed himself in very florid language and the imagery of the *Song of Solomon* was his delight. His writings, whether in meter or prose form, were not graphically illustrated and his instruction to the Brothers and Sisters in the writing school who were engaged in producing Fraktur-Schriften was to follow no set patterns and that each must work according to the dictates of his own spirit.

The Ephrata designs have furnished much speculation. Sachse, in various places, refers to *"the Ephrata Lily"* as if it were a definitely adopted symbol of the Ephrata Cloister, but he was evidently not very certain about the matter; for he finally calls the same design by the all-inclusive name of: "The mystical tulip, pomegranate and lily of Ephrata." What that may signify, I do not know.

I am disposed to think that certain general designs were naturally developed at Ephrata through the years, each designer, perhaps, more or less subconsciously following the other. Indeed, one who is familiar with Ephrata Manuscripts will be able to identify them from their general appearance as the product of the Cloister, and not because of designs emblematic or symbolical of religious teachings. Many of the Ephrata designs which include forms of tulips, pinks, lilies, geometrical and other conventional drawings on the same stalk or stem, would by some be thought of as the "tree of life." The whole thing is mere guess-work and interpretation at this time may or may not fit the designer's purpose.

Designs may be pictorial or illustrative; symbolical or interpretive; and conventional or decorative. In a *Catalog of an exhibition of Illuminated Manuscripts*, issued by the Pierpont Morgan Library (New York, 1933) it is pointed out that illumination proper is to be distinguished from illustration; the object of illumination being to beautify the object of devotion and of illustration to clarify it.

Our studies will be aided with a definition from Webster's *New International Dictionary*:

Symbol: That which stands for or suggests something else by reason of relationship, association, convention or accidental but not intentional resemblance especially. A visible sign of something invisible, as an idea, a quality, or totality such as a state or a church; an emblem as the lion is the symbol of courage; the cross is the symbol of Christianity.

As a part of history, it is an interesting fact that after the adoption of printing by movable type, the first purely German book was a collection of eighty-five fables, each with a German text of rhyming verses, printed in 1461.

Do Pennsylvania German Illuminated Manuscripts contain symbols of the occult? Do we find designs which have a mystical or magical implication? I make immediate answer, not by way of argument but as a definitive statement of that which I conceive to be the fact. I have examined hundreds of these manuscripts and I find that so far as they have any message to convey through design or symbol, it is distinctively religious in character. The truth intended to be taught in these manuscripts is to be found in the Bible and it does not lie in the occult. The symbols which are used typify Christianity and do not have a magical or pagan implication. They openly express the Christian faith and no one need look for symbols which indicate an unrevealed and subterranean faith in witchcraft and in influences that are weird.

There are those who have believed in the power of witches and in healing through pow-wowing. However, they do not proclaim their beliefs from the house-tops. Secrecy is the characteristic of their faith. They practice the Black arts (die Schwarze Kunst) and not the art of illumination. Their color is black and not the yellow, red and blue which so brilliantly lighten up the manuscripts in which we are interested.

Let us see what is meant by Christian symbolism and whether such symbols were used by the Pennsylvania Germans.

In *Symbolism in Religious Art*, Caryl Coleman states (New York, 1899):

"To the Primitive Christians, to the medieval Church builders, and the Christian artists of the Renaissance, symbolic forms and colors were as well known as the commercial symbols for dollars and cents are to us. In fact the representation of ideas by images and symbols was so common, their use in all forms of art so universal, that they became a sign or picture language familiar to all. By their means the uncultured, the most ignorant, could read in the sculptures and paintings, the colored windows and mosaics, with which the churches were so profusely adorned, the wisdom of God, the history of mankind and the beauty of holiness. In the sixteenth century, in the countries where the so-called new learning dominated, symbols, together with most of the outward symbols of religion, were done away with, because some of them it was said, had been perverted to superstitious uses."

W. H. Withrow in *The Catacombs of Rome* (Nelson & Philips, New York, 1877) says:—

"Primitive Christianity was eminently congenial to religious symbolism. Born in the east and in the bosom of Judaism, which had long been familiar with this universal oriental language, it adopted types and figures as its natural mode of expression. These formed the warp and woof of the symbolic drapery of the tabernacle and temple service, pre-figuring the great truths of the Gospel. The Old Testament sparkles with mysterious imagery. In the sublime visions of Isaiah, Ezekiel and Daniel, were strange creatures of wondrous form and prophetic significance. In the New Testament the Divine Teacher conveys the loftiest lessons in parables of immutable beauty. In the apocalyptic visions of St. John the language of imagery is exhausted to represent the overthrow of Satan, the triumph of Christ, and the glories of the New Jerusalem. The primitive therefore naturally adopted a similar mode of art expression for conveying religious instruction."

The religious faith of the Pennsylvania Germans, whatever differences there may be in the creeds of their various denominations and sects, includes three major beliefs:

1. The Fall of man from a perfect state. 2. Man's Redemption through Christ's sacrifice. 3. Salvation through faith and repentance. Inasmuch as the great purpose of Illuminated Manuscripts is religious in character, we may expect to find designs which symbolize these beliefs and which have been in use in Christian teaching during the centuries. Some of these manuscripts will now be referred to.

Adam and Eve are pictorially placed under a tree, with one or more apples. Sometimes the apple is in Eve's outstretched hand. The serpent is an expressionless spectator. In one specimen the apple rests on the serpent's head.

The *Baptism of Christ* properly is depicted in Baptismal certificates. Christ is usually standing in water, with the Baptist by his side and a dove descending from above.

Pictorial representations of *Christ on the Cross* are often met with. My copy of the *Martyrs Mirror*, printed at Ephrata, Pennsylvania, in 1748, has bound in a drawing or picture of the Crucifixion. It is delicately designed and embellished with quotations in Fraktur lettering of Biblical texts. There is a border of running vines in pale colors. At the base of the cross plants and trees are so drawn as to make them appear as if they were being blown by a mighty wind. There are columns on either side of the picture supporting a legend at the top. Color is sparingly used to mark the wounds in the body of Christ. The design as a whole is of the traditional type.

Angels make continuous appearances in these manuscripts. They generally are inartistically drawn and their shapes frequently provoke a smile. There may be an excuse for the curious shapes. Artists do not paint without models before them. Who ever saw an angel or the model of an angel? At any rate, angels are drawn in all attitudes—thin or fat; standing erect or on the wing from heaven to earth or from earth to heaven; now fully clad with long dresses which may expose clumsy shoes; and again with no garments saving their wings only. Angels' heads with wings are ever present. The imagination seems to have had fantastic deliverances in trying to solve the problems which angels always present. Let me not, however, be too facetious; for the Pennsylvania German did not experience a humorous but a religious sentiment when he thought of angels, however crudely the artist may have drawn the likeness. Does not the Psalmist declare that He shall give his angels charge of thee? Are not angels the messengers of God? Are they not in the company of the Redeemed singing never-ceasing praises to the Lamb? At times they carry in their hands a wreath, indicative of eternal life, or a sprig of olive symbolizing peace, or a palm pointing to victory.

There are specimens of portraiture of the *Madonna and Child* and with the *halo*, which suggests glorified light.

The *Cross* is used although not as frequently as one might suppose because of its primary importance in Christian symbology. I have found it in some of the Ephrata Manuscripts; in standards carried by a lamb; and in the outline of a heart.

In view of St. Paul's ringing declaration that there is laid up a crown of righteousness for such as love the Lord, frequent use is made of the *Crown*.

The *Lamb* is ever present as one of the great Christian symbols. It cannot be omitted from Christian teaching. Its use for sacrificial purposes in the days of the Old Dispensation; its simile as the Lamb of God which taketh away the sin of the world; and the place of the Lamb before the throne of God—all these have an irresistible appeal for the teacher and artists alike.

The *Dove* appears in the manuscripts without number for decorative and symbolical purposes. The dove has always been an attractive bird. In pagan art doves draw the chariot of Venus and from the oaks of Dodona doves uttered the oracles of the future. The dove was the celestial messenger of Mahomet. It was marked in early Biblical days as Noah's messenger, and was offered as a sacrifice. Since the Spirit of God descended like a dove upon Christ after his baptism, the dove has a definite place in Christian symbolism.

The *Lily* and the *Rose* are used for symbolical purposes. It is evident, however, that the artists were thinking of American lilies and roses and not the botanical varieties which grew in Palestine. How can any teacher and artist resist the great texts dealing with the Rose of Sharon and with the Lilies of the field?

From the animal kingdom pictorially appear the *Serpent*, the *Hart* (or Deer), the *Peacock* and the *Eagle*. From the terrestrial world the artists appropriated for the purposes of illustration, the *sun*, the *moon*, the *stars*, the *rainbow*. All of these may have no particular value as ecclesiastical symbols but they have a permanent place in the Biblical text.

We have now reached the borderland between symbolism, poetic suggestion and decoration. Technical ecclesiastical symbolism is one thing and the play of the imagination applying simile and metaphor is another.

In the manuscripts we find drawings of *parrots, crocodiles, mermaids, pelicans*. Some of these have no religious symbolical value. Others had a mythological significance.

An interesting illustration of the growth of symbolism is found in the *Pelican* which was an unclean bird according to Leviticus. Thompson in *The Land and the Book* says it is a solitary bird and the very picture of desolation, giving great depth of meaning to the Psalmists' declaration: "I am like a pelican of the wilderness." Thompson says the bird is as large as a half grown donkey and when it settles on its stout legs it looks like one. How differently it appears in legendary lore! About A.D. 1260 a friar named Bartholomew Anglicus wrote a manuscript on the properties of things referred to under the title of *De Proprietatibus Rerum*. Abstracts of this manuscript were published in London (1893) under the title of *Medieval Lore*. The author gives the physical properties of "things" and in many cases also their symbolical meanings. Of the *Pelican* he says:

> "Master Jacobus de Vitriaco in his book of the wonders of the Eastern parts telleth a cause of the death of pelicans' birds. He saith that the serpent hateth kindly this bird. Wherefore when the mother passeth out of the nest to get meat, the serpent climbeth on the tree, and stingeth and infecteth the birds. And when the mother cometh again, she maketh sorrow three days for her birds, as it is said. Then she smiteth herself in the breast and springeth blood upon them, and reareth them from death to life, and then for great bleeding the mother waxeth feeble, and the birds are compelled to pass out of the nest to get themselves meat. And some of them for kind love feed the mother that is feeble, and some are unkind and care not for the mother, and the mother taketh good heed thereto, and when she cometh to her strength, she nourisheth and loveth those birds that fed her in her need, and putteth away her other birds, as unworthy and unkind, and suffereth them not to dwell nor live with her."

Christian art finally adopted the pelican as a symbol of Christ. As there is ascribed to the pelican the act of tearing open her breast and the giving of blood to her young, it has become the emblem of redemption through the sufferings and death of Christ.

It is difficult to determine whether the *Peacock* was used as a symbol. Its history as a symbol is interesting. Job (Ch. 39:13) asks: "Gavest thou the goodly wings to a peacock?" Withrow in the publication already quoted says that the peacock was the proud bird of Juno. In early Christian art the peacock is an emblem of immortality and only in later days did he become the symbol of pride. The reader may assign what symbolical meaning he pleases. It has true decorative value as appears in Plate No. 21 where the peacock forms an integral portion of the letter D.

Passing through the field of true symbolism and the borderland of symbolism, we reach designs which are purely decorative. Those interested in symbolism may consult the *Handbook of Legendary and Mythological Art* by Clara Erskine Clement (Boston 1881).

Charles Rufus Morey in a remarkably analytical and searching introduction to a *Catalog of an Exhibition of Illuminated Manuscripts* by the Pierpont Morgan Library held at the New York Public Library (1933) says:

> "Gothic art is the expression of Latin Christianity in human terms, and was thus fraught from the start with a dual purpose, in its human interest on the one hand, and its profound religious feeling on the other. . . . No Gothic artist questioned whether this or that was worth depicting or adorning; if it belonged to the world which God created, it was something that had ultimate significance and charm. Ugly or fair, great or small, noble or mean—everything had its place in the Divine Scheme; and once that place was realized or marked, the Gothic art enshrined it in a poetry that is no more spontaneous and reverent when it enriched a cathedral than when it lighted up the pages of a book."

In the *Chronicon Ephratense* (Ephrata 1786), as has already been quoted, no one in the writing-school was permitted to borrow a design anywhere for Beissel their leader said, "We dare not borrow from each other, because *the power to produce rests within everybody*."

Let us look at a few of the outstanding designs, drawings and pictures which are ever present and which add life and even gayety to the manuscripts.

Parrots appear singly and even in pairs in the same drawing. So far as I know, they have no symbolical value whatever. They do have a decorative value because of the opportunity of using brilliant colors in profusion.

A *crocodile,* eight inches long and evenly colored with a brilliant red, is drawn at the bottom of a Baptismal Certificate in my possession. There is probably no symbolism in its use—not even to illustrate "crocodile tears." In *De Proprietatibus Rerum*, above referred to, the author writes:

> "If the crocodile findeth a man by the brim of the water, or by the cliff, he slayeth him if he may, and then he weepeth upon him, and swalloweth him at the last."

Mermaids, not only in traditional shapes, but also with twisted tails, on occasion, adorn Baptismal Certificates. Let me dispose of its symbolical value by again quoting from *De Proprietatibus Rerum*:

> "The mermaid is a sea beast wonderly shapen, and draweth shipmen to peril by sweetness of song. The Gloss on Is. xiii saith that sirens are serpents with crests. And some men say, that they are fishes of the sea in likeness of women. Some men feign that there are three Sirens some-seal maidens, and some-deal fowls with claws and wings, and one of them singeth with voice, and another with a pipe, and the third with an harp, and they please so shipmen, with likeness of song, that they draw them to peril and to shipbreach, but the sooth is that they drew men that passed by them to poverty and to mischief."

In Plates No. 21 and No. 25 two doves are united, breast with breast. In Brumbaugh's *Life of Dock* there is a plate which shows the tails of two doves intertwined. I find nothing in symbology to explain the significance of that union. It is easy, however, to surmise a number of things. The most evident one is that it is purely decorative. Union by interwining tail feathers lacks poetry. As already indicated the descending dove directs our thought to the spirit of God. The flight of a dove out of the mouth of a dying person has been used as a symbol of the flight of the soul. The pictured union of two doves might, therefore, be said to indicate the union of the soul of man with the spirit of God. What the penman who drew the designs meant is pure conjecture.

THE TULIP

The general impression is that the *Tulip* is the one flower used by Pennsylvania German Penmen. Its use as a decoration of manuscripts, furniture and pottery is frequent but by no means exclusive of other flowers, as has been noted in the section on designs. Symbolically it has been said to be emblematic of the Trinity. By reason of the general flowering of the tulip in Pennsylvania German gardens and its uses in art, let us make a brief inquiry into the botanical structure of the plant and its history.

The Pennsylvania German name of the tulip may be conveyed by the following words, which are spelled phonetically: Dulleban; Dol-le-bawn; Dul-le-bawn. It appears that the word tulip is derived from the Persian *dulband* (turban) which gradually was pronounced *tulband*.

Botanically the perianth of the tulip consists of six petals which are arranged in two sets of three, the outer one differing somewhat in shape from the inner. The flower has six stamens consisting of large anthers set endwise upon filaments springing from the base of the flower. Occasionally, however, the flower is arranged in fours instead of threes and we find two sets of four petals each, eight stamens and a quadripartite ovary.

In 1561 Conrad Gessner wrote a description of the gardens in Germany and he refers to the introduction of the tulip, as follows:

"In the month of April 1559, in the garden of the Great Councillor, John Henry Herwart, I saw this plant displayed, sprung from a seed which had come from Constantinople, or, as others say, from Cappadocia. It was flowering with a single beautifully red flower, large, like a red lilly, formed of eight petals of which four were outside and the rest within. It had a very sweet, soft and subtle scent which soon disappeared."

In a book written by A. Daniel Hall, entitled *The Book of the Tulip* (Stokes & Co., New York 1928) there is a summary of its place in Europe:

"The tulip, universally as it is now grown in our gardens, cannot properly be regarded as a European flower. The home of the genus is the uplands near the headwaters of the Euphrates and Tigris, from Asia Minor into Persia, and though one or two species are probably true natives of Greece and Turkey in Europe, tulips did not make their appearance in Western gardens until the sixteenth century. . . . As far as can be ascertained the tulip was unknown in Western Europe before the middle of the sixteenth century. The negative evidence is considerable. In the first place there is no mention of such a flower in any of the earlier lists of plants or in general literature, yet it is unlikely that so attractive a flower would have escaped notice. When the flower was introduced from Turkey it was hailed by all the botanists and gardeners of the time as something unlike any of the plants with which they were acquainted. . . . Another significant circumstance is that as far as has been ascertained no representation of a tulip occurs in pictures or in miniatures prior to the known introduction of the garden tulip. The Florentine and many of the early German painters were very fond of placing flowers in the foreground of their pictures, often drawn with great care and precision so that they can be identified with certainty. But though I have kept my eyes open for many years now, neither in the chief European galleries nor in photographs have I seen anything, even among the merely stylised flowers, that would suggest a tulip."

When the tulip was introduced into Europe, great interest was being taken in gardens throughout Germany and in the Low Countries and in England; less so in France. Tulip culture developed rapidly and the tulip became an article of commerce and speculation. Hall observes that we read of them in Belgium in 1583; in Leyden in 1590; in Middleburg in 1596; in Montpelier in 1598; and in Lucerne in 1599. Also that evidence of the rapid spread of the fashion may be seen in the well-known picture at Munich of Rubens walking in his garden with Helen Fourment, his second wife. The flower beds are set out with a number of tulips, yet the date of the picture is about 1632. The high prices and the ease with which a profit might be made on the increase by offsets led to speculation, which suddenly rose to a fever-heat in the years of the tulip mania, 1634-37. Bulbs were sold by auction and all classes of people in Holland entered into the gamble, for it had become a public gamble, in which bulbs were sold and resold for a rise while they were still in the ground. These speculations finally brought about a financial panic in which there were tremendous losses.

I have gone through the various hymn-books used by the Pennsylvania German Pioneers. Nowhere do I find the tulip used in a symbolical sense. In fact, I have only seen it referred to in two instances and then it is mentioned with other flowers. In the *Weyrauchs Hugel* (Germantown 1739) in the hymn on page 218, the author asks where he may find Him whom he loves. He looks to nature and in beautiful poetic language he refers to the tulip, narcissus, lily, rose, hyacinth, violet and flowers in general.

My studies have led me to the conclusion that the tulip was used for decorative purposes only and that it is not a symbol of the Trinity.

Conclusion

AND now in conclusion—a melodious phrase, often heard issuing out of the mouths of public speakers, who, in spite of the utterance, persist in the errors of their way. The writing of this section, though brief, has been beset with all the difficulties of a labyrinth. In my efforts to reach conclusions, I was constantly embarrassed with the admonition that the end was at hand.

The studies recorded in this monograph have behind them years of collecting during which the spirit of the quest grew and grew until it has become impossible to distinguish between a barnacle and this pernicious but pleasure-giving habit. Be it said, however, that collecting is attended with unexpected compensations. Thus, I must confess, that my interest in Paul the Apostle is heightened because of the fact that he, too, was a collector of books and manuscripts. As he went on a journey, he put his treasures in storage and then (as all collectors would do) sighed for his adopted waifs until one day he charged his beloved Timothy thus:

> "The cloke that I left at Troas with Carpus, when thou comest, bring with thee, and the books, but especially the parchments."

I trust that the reader of this monograph has been impressed with the fact that in its preparation, I have had in mind the suggestion made by Sir Thomas Browne that "a great deal of conscience should go into the making of a history."

Much remains to be said and I hope that that which has been said will be such as to lead others to say it.

The use of superlatives and expressions of admiration have been studiously avoided in the text. Lest I be thought to be a mere fact-finding investigator, let me now make amends by hanging all Pennsylvania German Illuminated Manuscripts in the Temple of Beauty. As I do so, I hear the immortal voice of the poet Keats:

> "A thing of beauty is a joy forever:
> Its loveliness increases; it will never
> Pass into nothingness; but still will keep
> A bower quiet for us, and a sleep
> Full of sweet dreams, and health, and quiet breathing."

Upon the completion of his work in Monastic days, the calligrapher frequently made bold to add a closing word of his own. One Johannes at "Weysselstorff" craved a blessing (as I do) at the close of a manuscript, dated A.D. 1444:

> Hie hat diez buch ein ent;
> Gott uns seinen gotlichen segen sent.
> Explicit expliciunt—
> Sprach die katz zu dem hund:
> Biszt du mich,
> So kratz ich dich.

REPRODUCTIONS

Pennsylvania German Illuminated Manuscripts

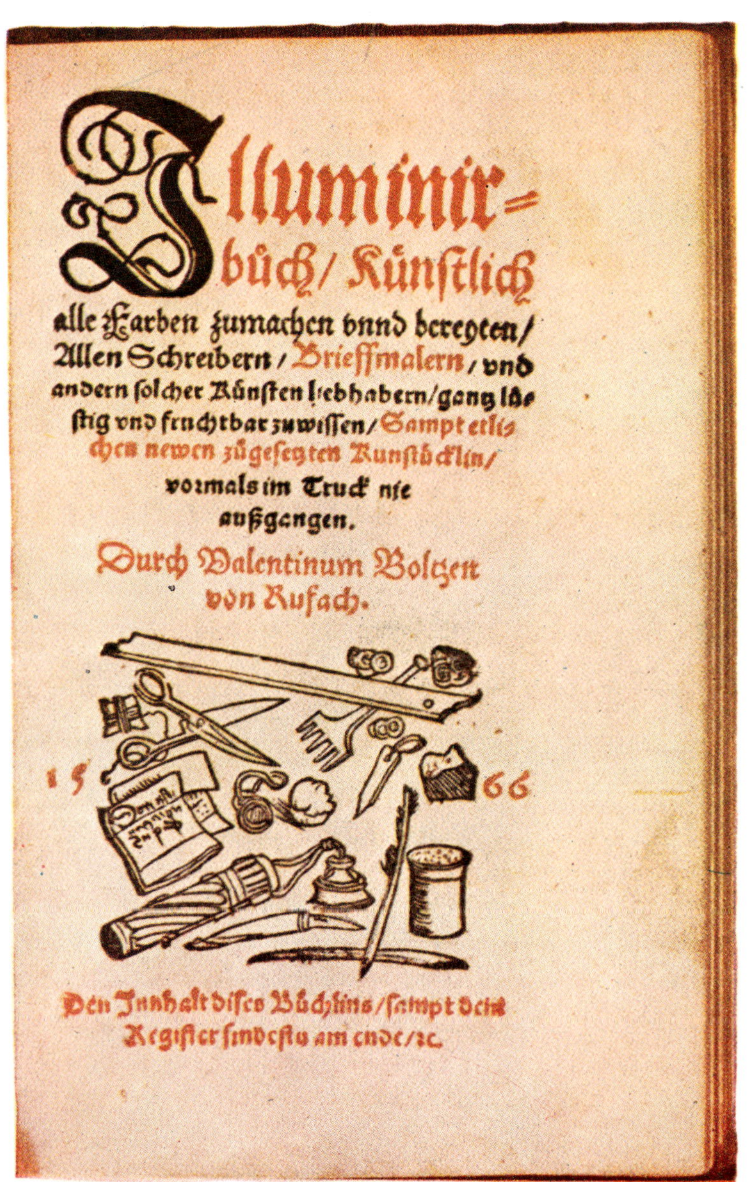

Illuminir=
bůch/ Künstlich
alle Farben zumachen vnnd bereyten/
Allen Schreibern/ Brieffmalern/ vnd
andern solcher Künsten liebhabern/ gantz lü=
stig vnd fruchtbar zuwissen/ Sampt etli=
chen newen zůgesetzten Kunstücklin/
vormals im Truck nie
außgangen.
Durch Valentinum Boltzen
von Rufach.

15 66

Den Innhalt dises Büchlins/ sampt dem
Register findestu am ende/ etc.

1. Title Page of the *Illuminirbuch* by Valentin Boltzen of Rufach, 1566 (title transcribed and translated on page 41).

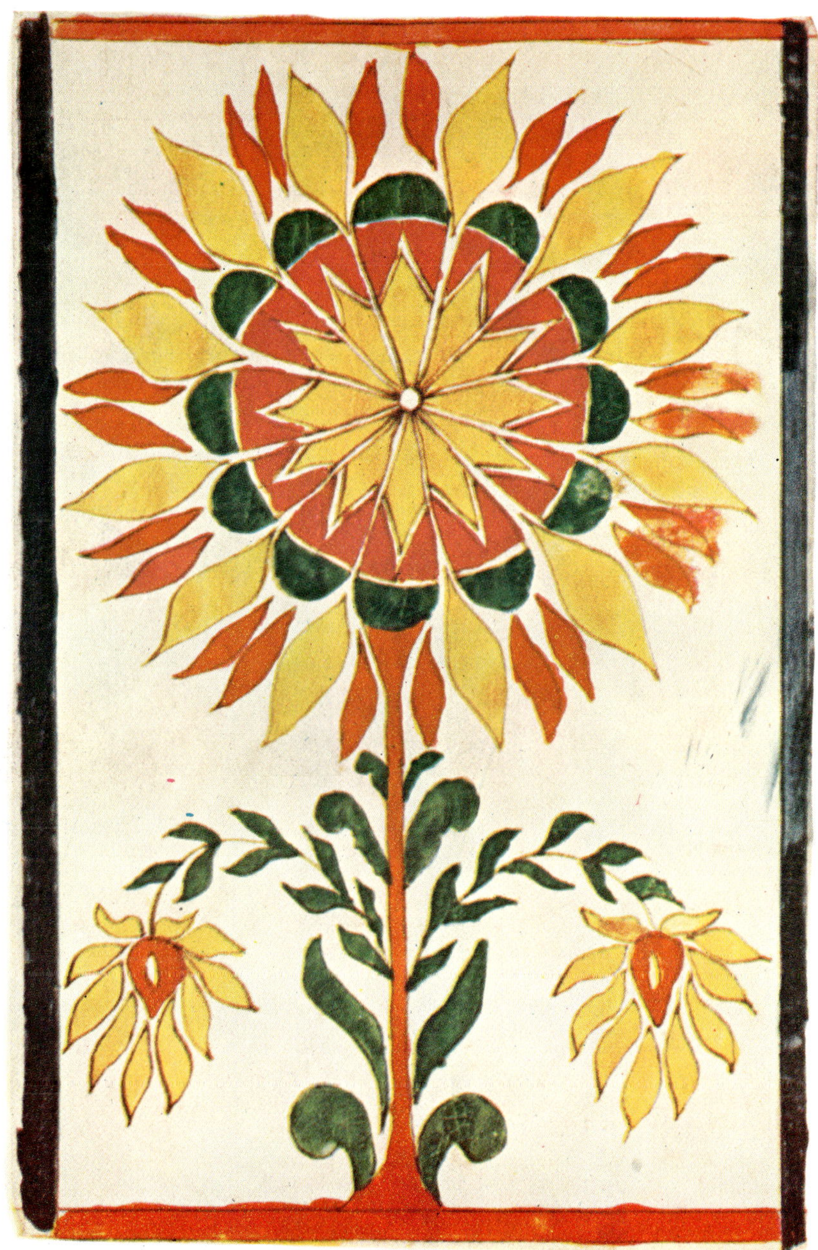

2. Freehand color design. The design is unrestrained and color combinations are brilliant. The name of the artist does not appear. The probable date is 1825.

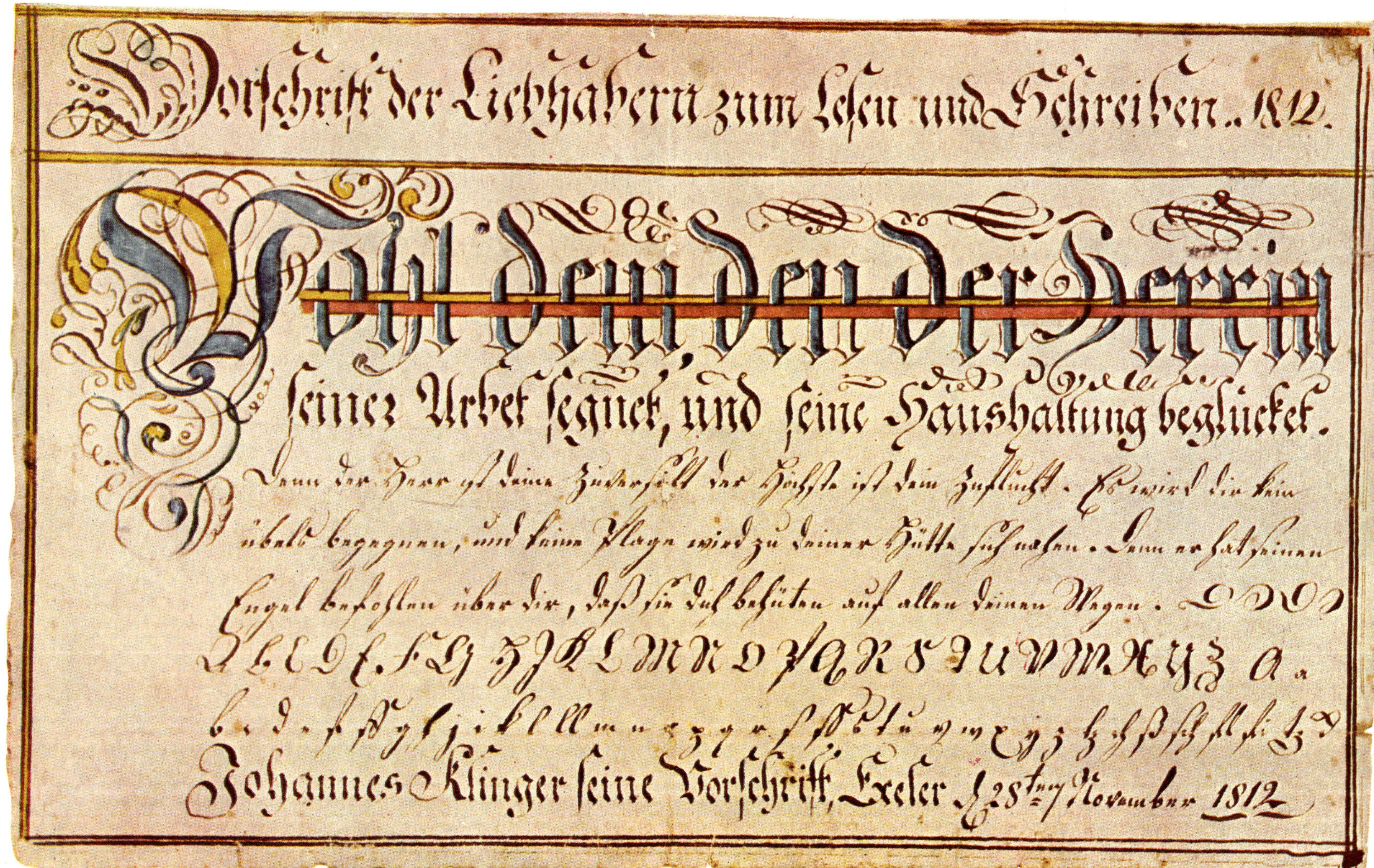

Vorschrift der Liebhabern zum Lesen und Schreiben. 1812.

Wohl dem den der Herr in seiner Arbet segnet, und seine Haushaltung beglücket.

Johannes Klinger seine Vorschrift, Exeter d 28ten November 1812

3. Vorschrift, by Johannes Klinger of Exeter, dated November 28, 1812. A specimen of calligraphy and illumination, intended, as its heading states, for those who have a love for reading and writing (see page 10). The text begins: "Wohl dem, den der Herr in seiner Arbet segnet, und seine Haushaltung beglücket" (Fortunate is he whose work is blessed and whose household is prospered by the Lord). Manuscripts of this class usually close with the letters of the German alphabet and numerals from 1 to 10.

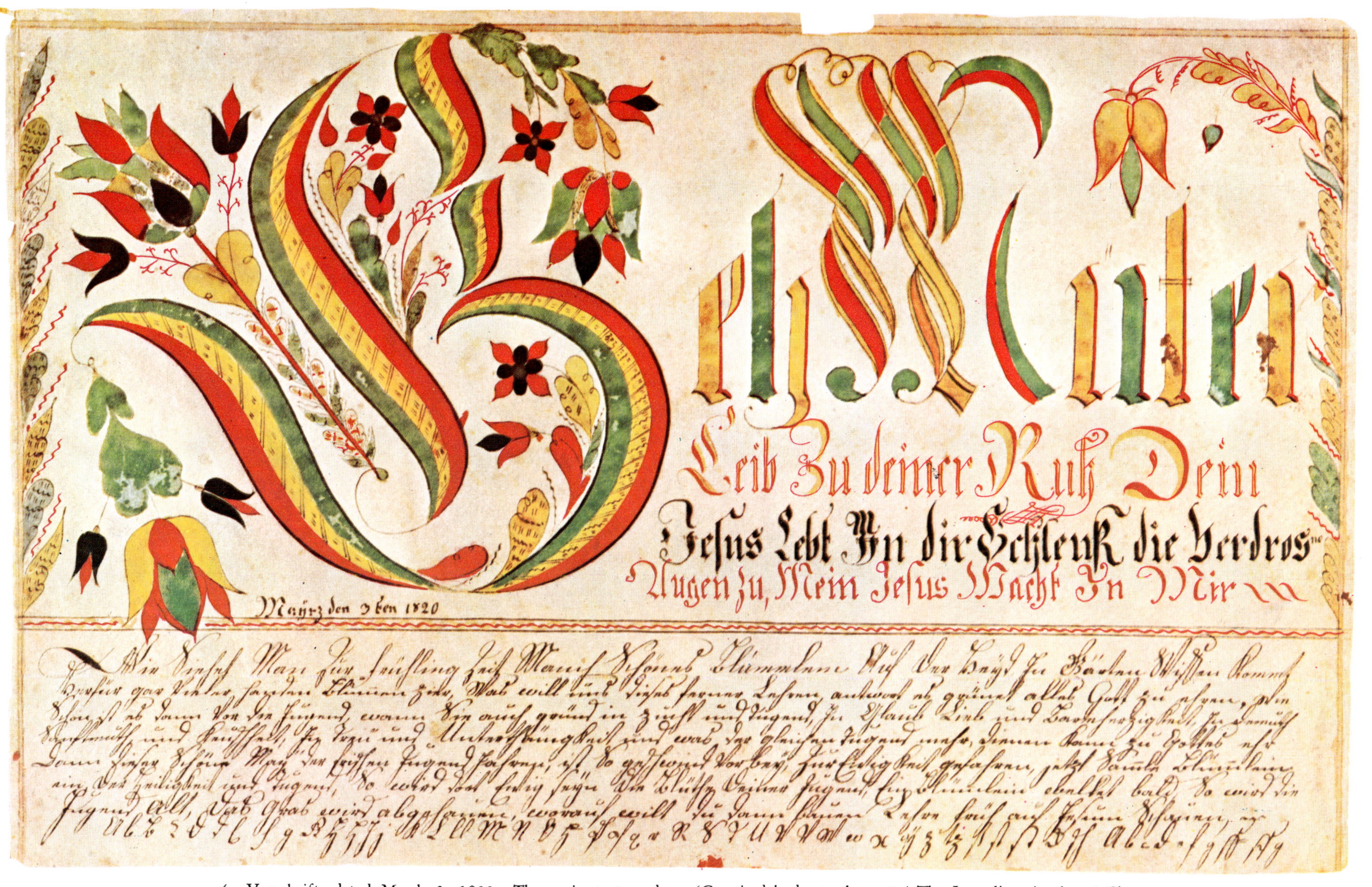

4. Vorschrift, dated March 3, 1820. The main text reads: "Geh Müter Leib Zu deiner Ruh/ Dein Jesus lebt In dir/ Schleusz die Verdros^ne Augen zu,/ Mein Jesus Wacht In Mir" (Go, tired body, to thy rest,/ Thy Jesus lives in thee./ Close thy drowsy eyes,/ My Jesus watches in me).

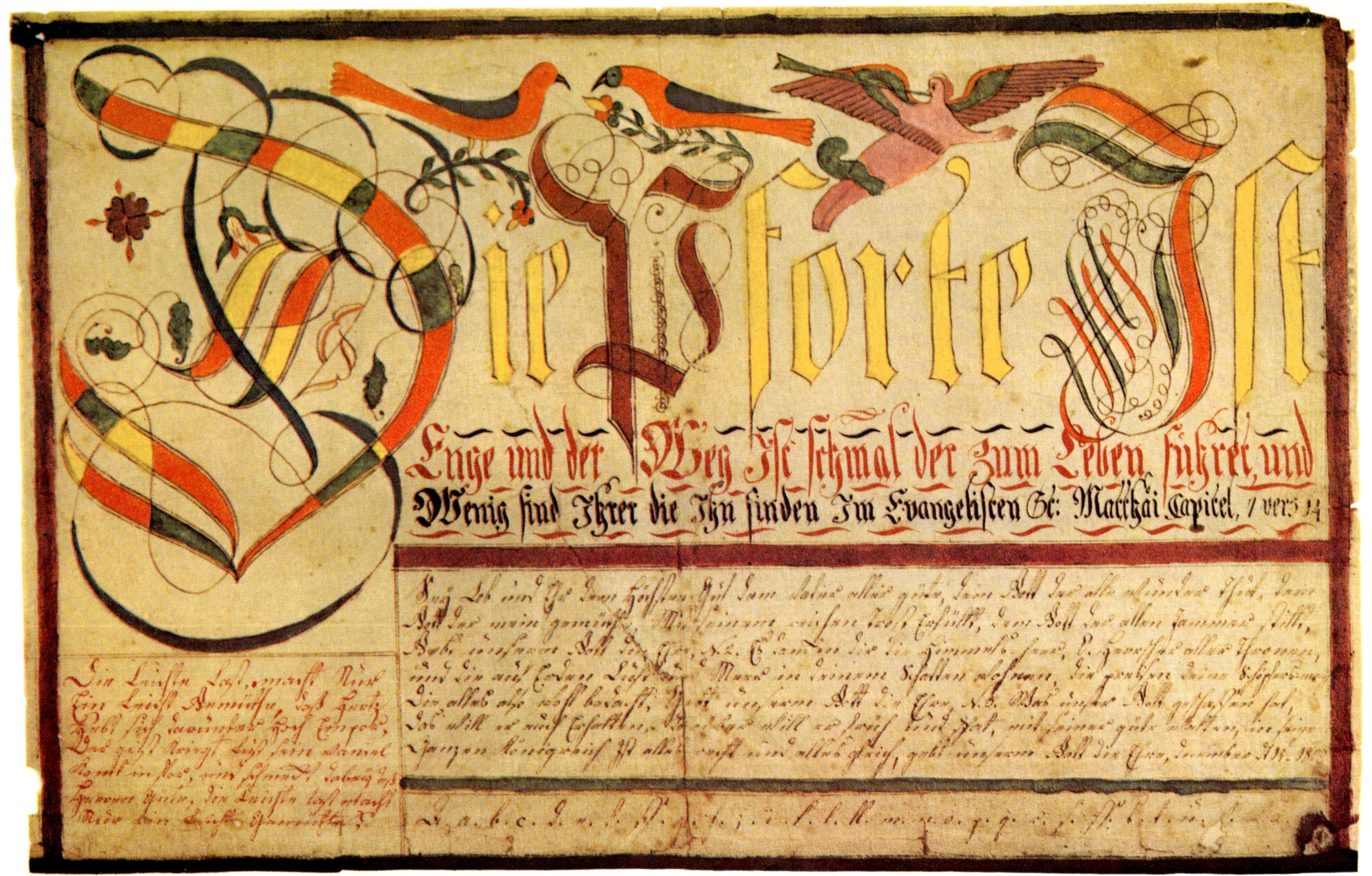

5. Vorschrift, dated December 23, 1808. The main text reads: "Die Pforte Ist Enge und der Weg Ist schmal der zum Leben führet, und Wenig sind Ihrer die Ihn finden Im Evangelisten St. Matthäi Capitel, 7 vers 14" (Strait is the gate and narrow is the way which leadeth unto life and few those be that find it: Mathew 7:14).

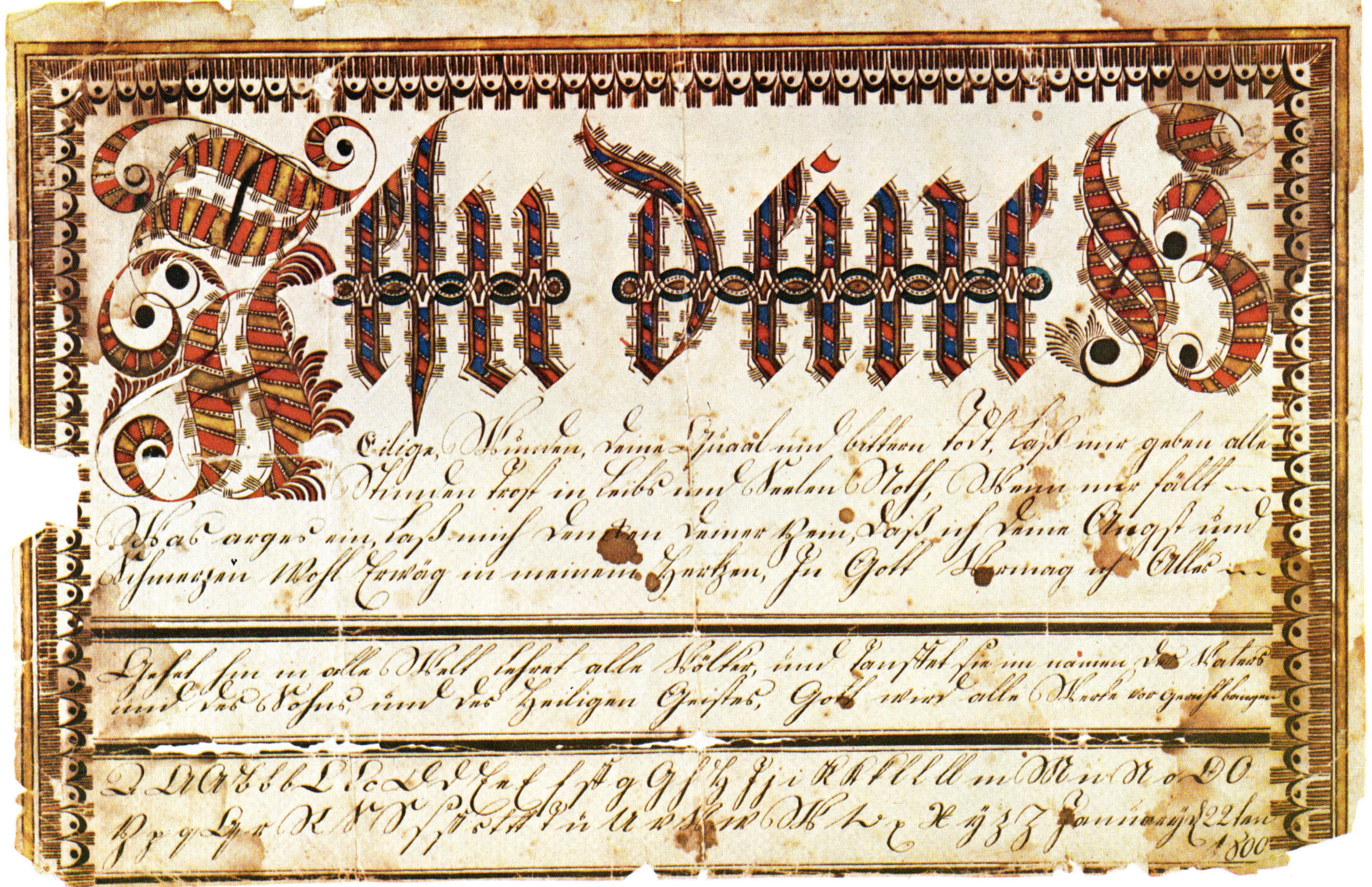

6. Vorschrift, dated January 22, 1800. The text begins: "Jesu deine Heilige Wunden,/ deine Quaal und bittere Todt,/ lasz mir geben alle Stunden/ trost in Leibs und Seelen Noth" (Jesus, Thy holy wounds,/ Thy torment and bitter death:/ Let me in all hours have/ Consolation when distressed in body and soul).

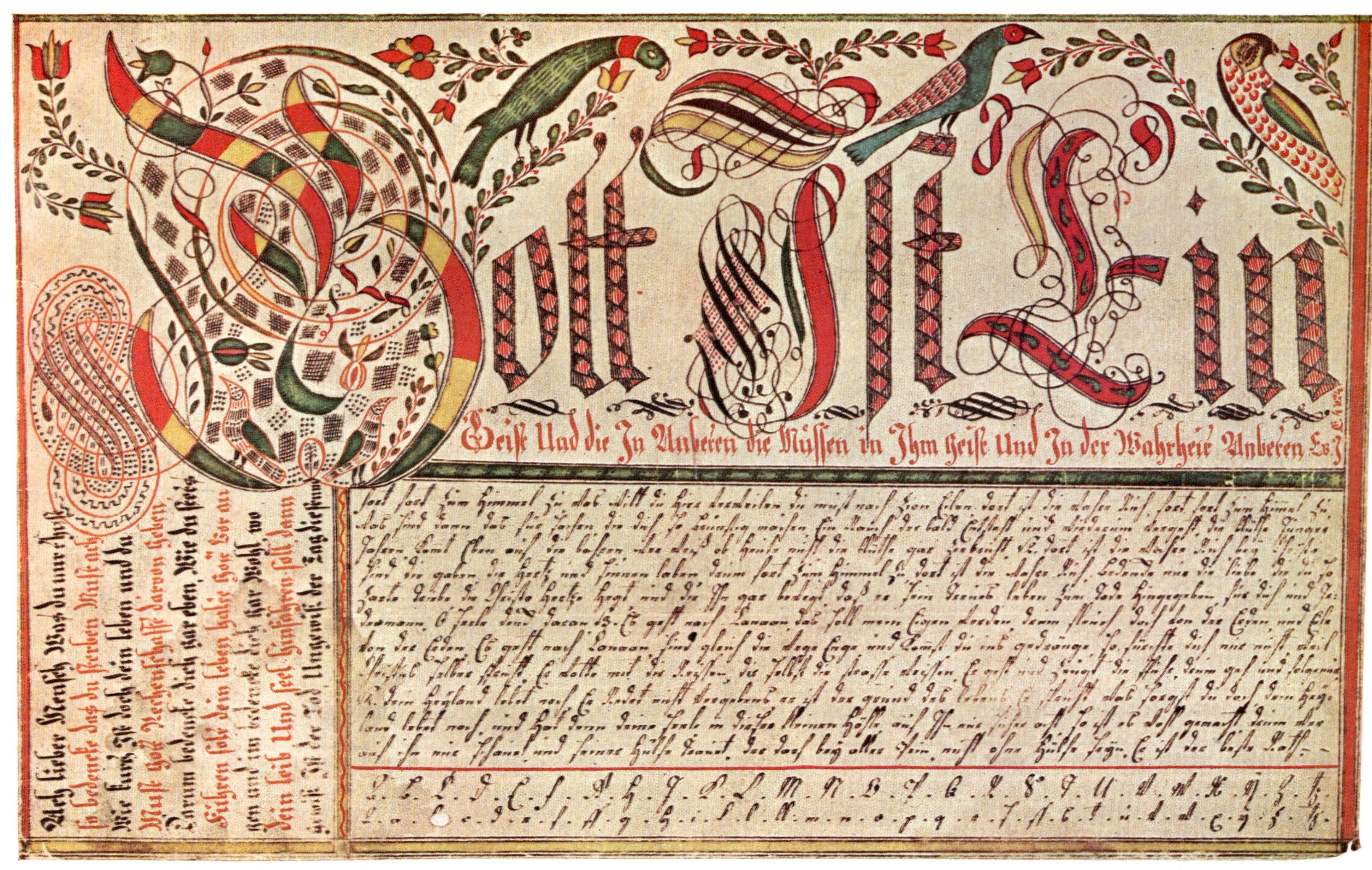

7. Vorschrift. The main text reads: "Gott Ist Ein Geist Und die In Anbeten die Müssen in Ihm Geist Und In der Wahrheit Anbeten Ev. J C. 4 v 24" (God is a spirit and they that worship Him must worship Him in spirit and in truth: John 4:24).

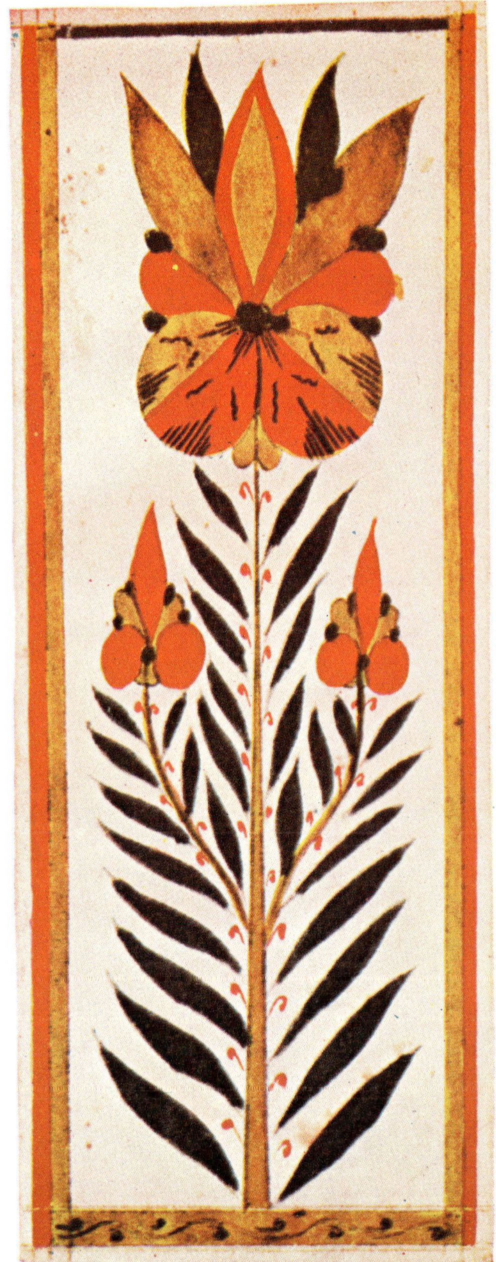

8. Color design. Because these small designs are frequently found in books, they have been termed book marks.

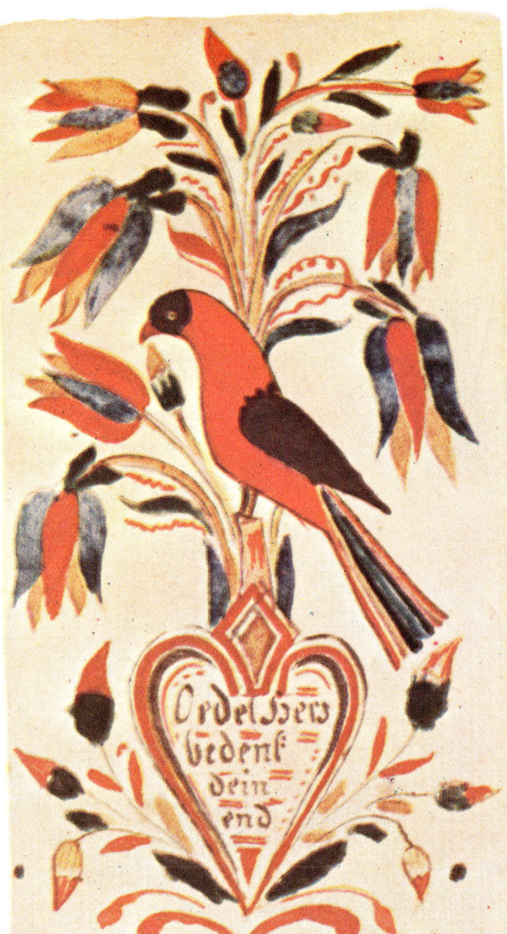

9. Color design and precept. Text: "O edel Herz bedenk dein end" (O noble heart, bethink thy end).

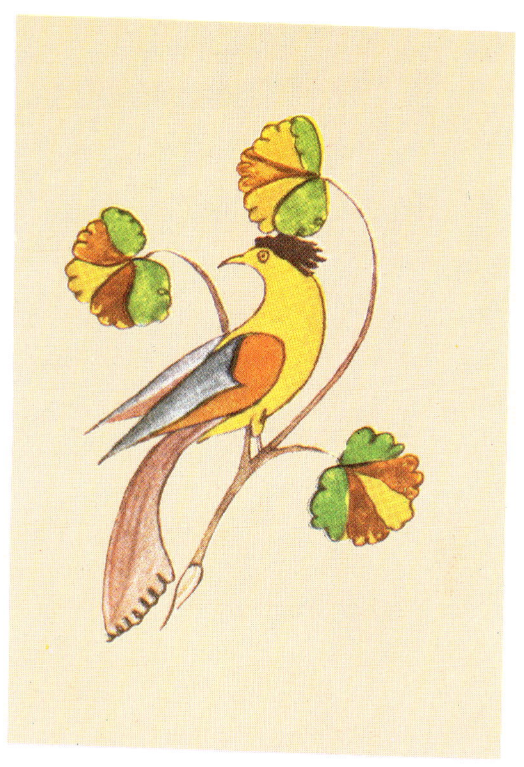

10. Color design.

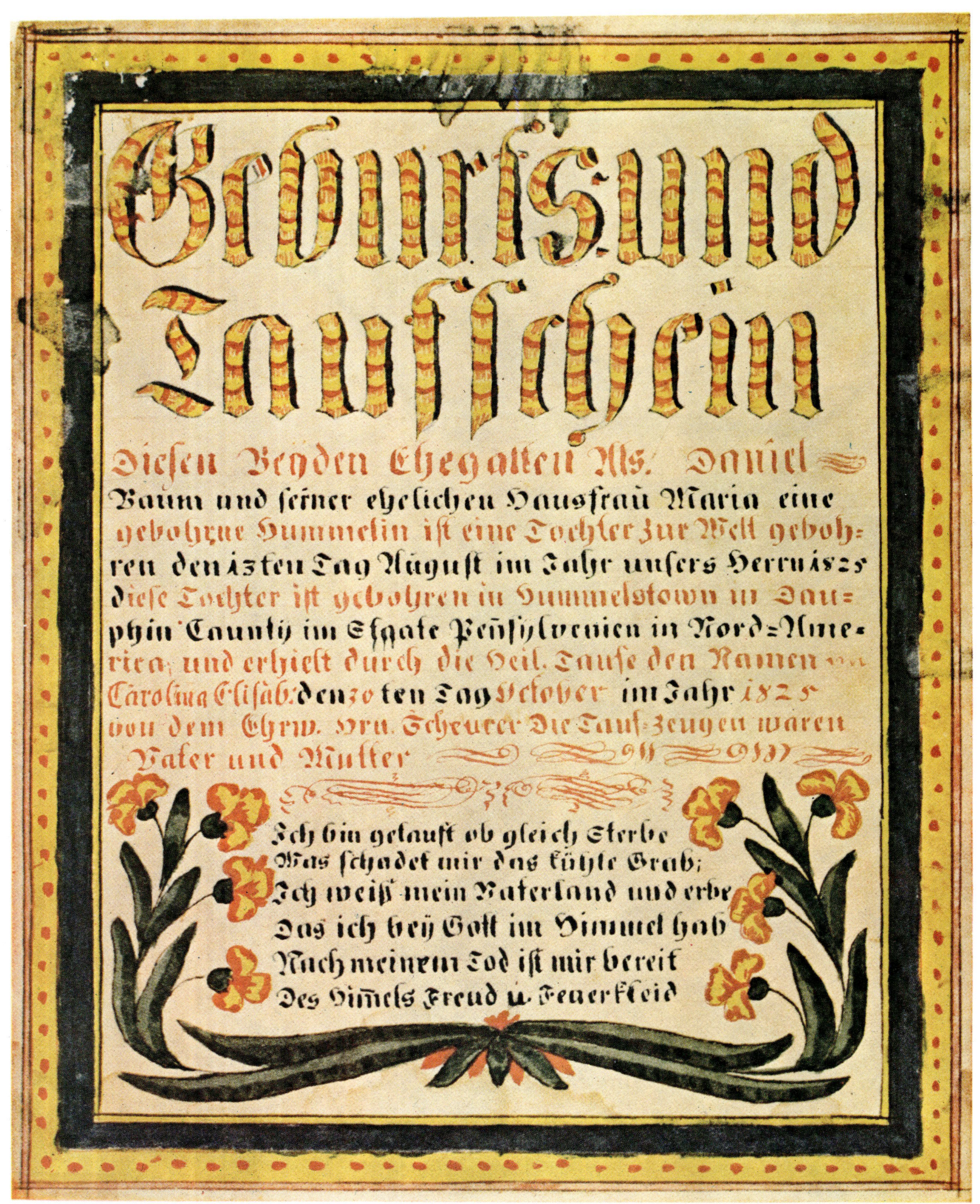
Geburts und Taufschein

Diesen Beyden Ehegatten Als. Daniel
Baum und seiner ehelichen Hausfrau Maria eine
gebohrne Hummelin ist eine Tochter zur Welt gebohren den 13ten Tag August im Jahr unsers Herrn 1825
diese Tochter ist gebohren in Hummelstown in Dauphin County im Staate Peñsylvenien in Nord-America, und erhielt durch die Heil. Taufe den Namen
Carolina Elisab. den 30 ten Tag October im Jahr 1825
von dem Ehrw. Hrn. Scheurer Die Tauf-Zeugen waren
Vater und Mutter

Ich bin getauft ob gleich Sterbe
Was schadet mir das kühle Grab;
Ich weiß mein Vaterland und erbe
Das ich bey Gott im Himmel hab
Nach meinem Tod ist mir bereit
Des Himels Freud u. Feuerkleid

11. Birth and baptismal certificate. This certificate labels itself as: "Geburts- und Taufschein." It records the birth on August 13 and baptism on October 30, 1825, of Carolina Elisabeth Baum, Hummelstown, Dauphin County.

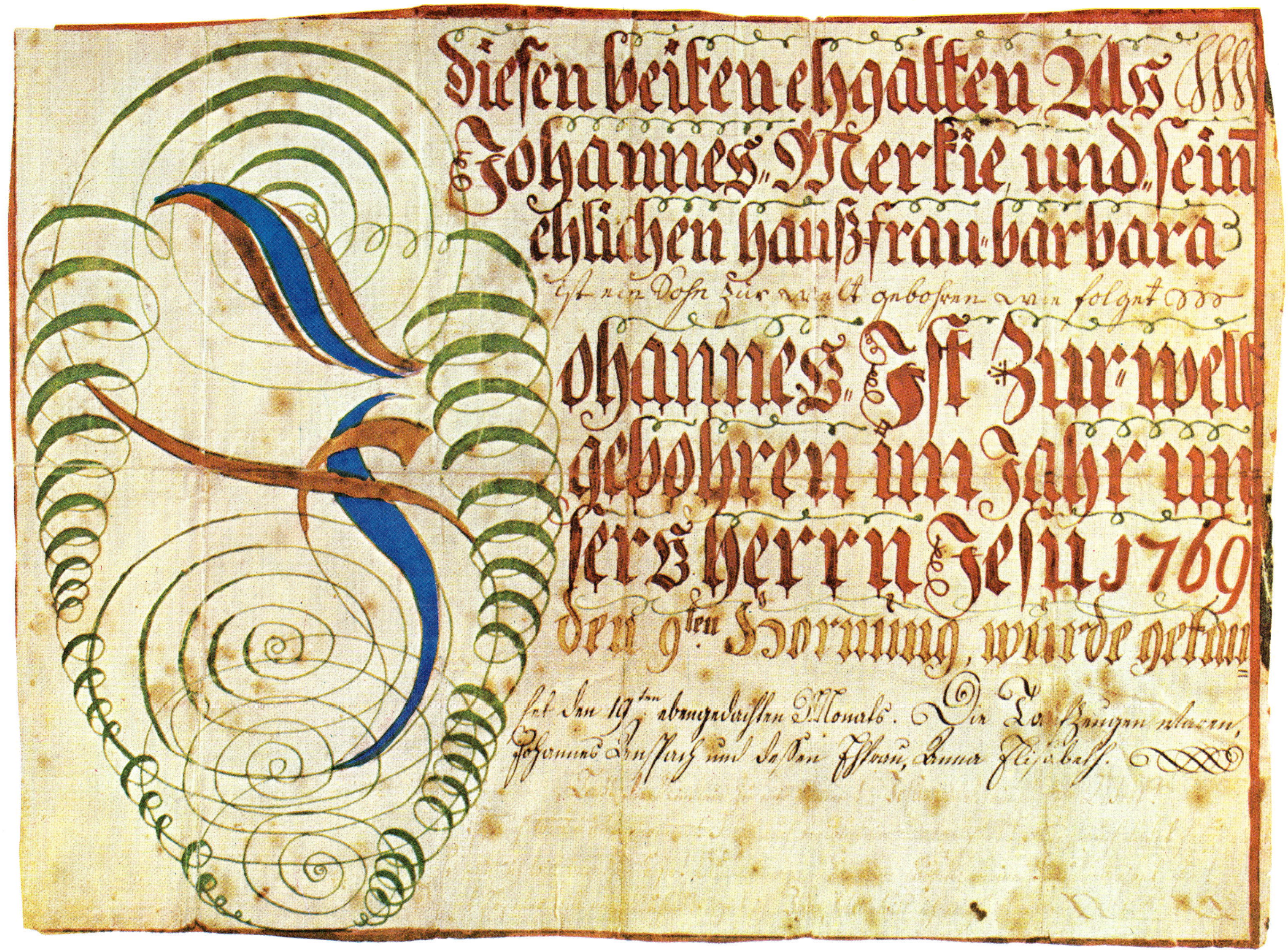

Diesen beiten ehgalten Als
Johannes Merkie und sein
ehlichen haußfrau barbara
Johannes Ist Zur welt
gebohren im Jahr un
sers herrn Jesu 1769
den 9ten Horning, würde getau

12. Birth and baptismal certificate. It records the birth on February 9 and baptism on February 19, 1769, of Johannes Merkie. The design of the initial letter J, with its strong color contrasts of green and blue, is noteworthy.

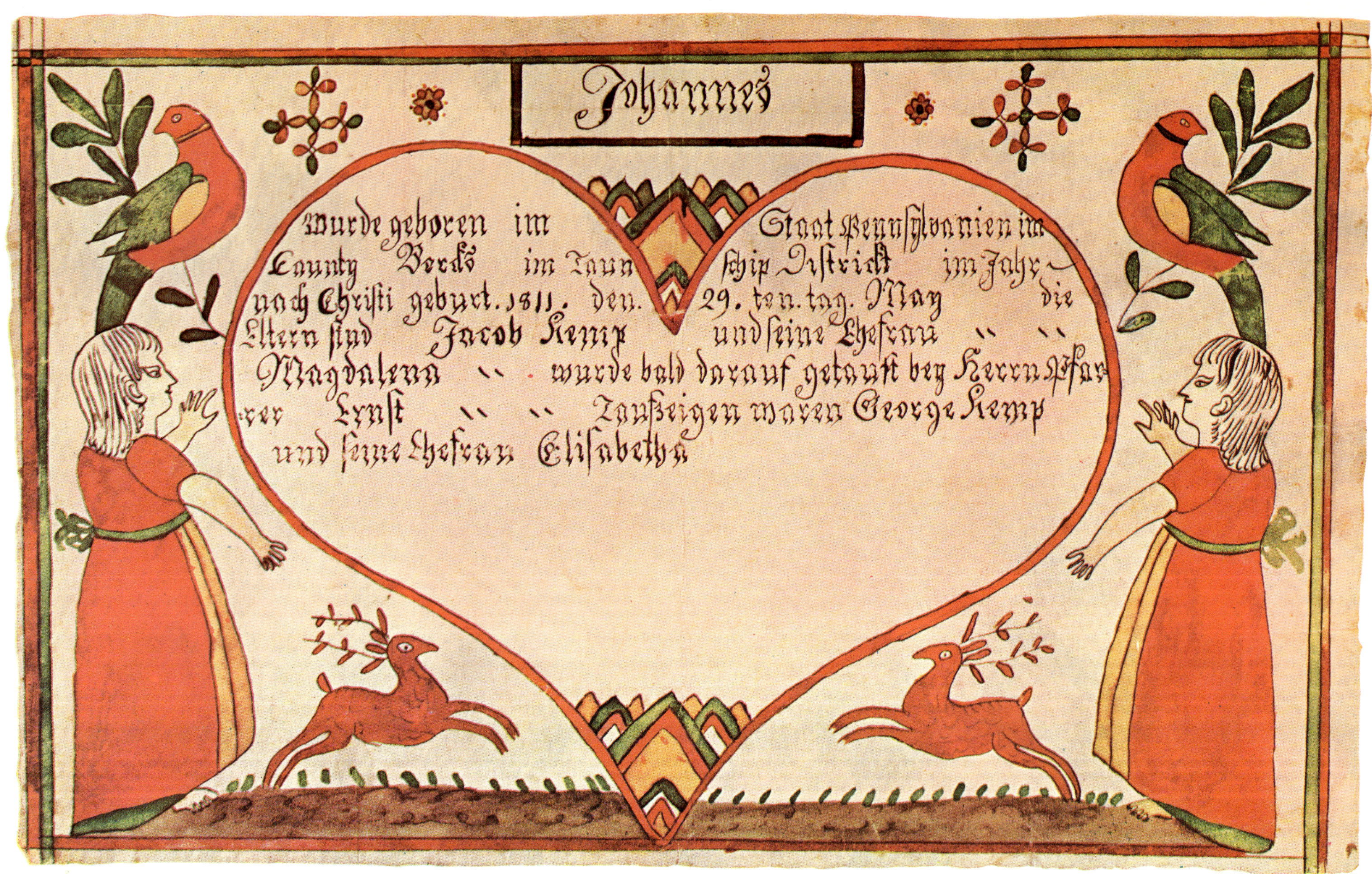

Johannes

wurde geboren im Staat Pennsylvanien im
County Berks im Taun schip Districkt im Jahr
nach Christi geburt. 1811. den 29. ten. tag. May die
Eltern sind Jacob Kemp und seine Ehefrau
Magdalena wurde bald darauf getauft bey Herrn Pfar-
-rer Ernst Taufzeigen waren George Kemp
und seine Ehefrau Elisabetha

13. Birth and baptismal certificate. It records the birth and baptism on May 29, 1811, of Johannes Kemp, Berks County.

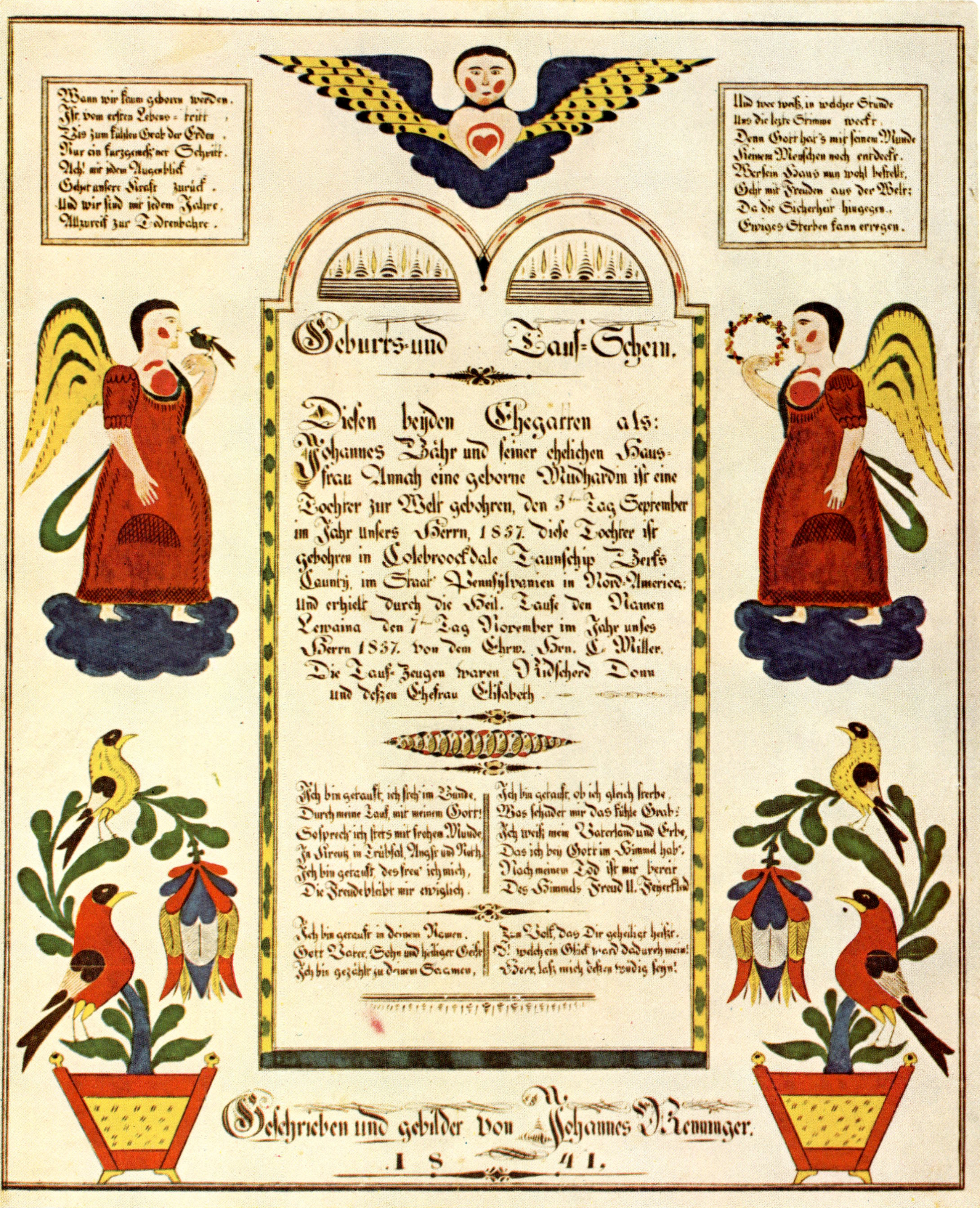

Wann wir kaum gebohrn werden.
Ist, vom ersten Lebens = tritt ,
Bis zum kühlen Grab der Erden .
Nur ein kurzgemess'ner Schritt .
Ach! mit jedem Augenblick
Gehet unsere Kraft zurück .
Und wir sind mit jedem Jahre ,
Allzureif zur Todtenbahre .

Und wer weiß, in welcher Stunde
Uns die lezte Stimme weckt ,
Denn Gott hat's mit seinem Munde
Keinem Menschen noch entdeckt .
Wer sein Haus nun wohl bestellt ,
Geht mit Freuden aus der Welt:
Da die Sicherheit hingegen ..
Ewiges Sterben kann erregen .

Geburts-und Tauf-Schein.

Diesen beyden Ehegatten als:
Johannes Bähr und seiner ehelichen Hausfrau Annah eine geborne Mudhardin ist eine Tochter zur Welt gebohren, den 3ten Tag September im Jahr unsers Herrn, 1837. diese Tochter ist gebohren in Colebroockdale Taunschip Berks Caunty, im Staat Pennsylvanien in Nord-America; Und erhielt durch die Heil. Taufe den Namen Lewaina den 7ten Tag November im Jahr unses Herrn 1837. von dem Ehrw. Hrn. C. Miller. Die Tauf-Zeugen waren Ridschord Donn und deßen Ehefrau Elisabeth .

Ich bin getauft, ich steh' im Bunde,
Durch meine Tauf, mit meinem Gott!
So sprech' ich stets mit frohem Munde,
In Kreutz in Trübsal, Angst und Noth,
Ich bin getauft, des freu' ich mich,
Die Freude bleibt mir ewiglich .

Ich bin getauft, ob ich gleich sterbe ,
Was schadet mir das kühle Grab:
Ich weiß mein Vaterland und Erbe,
Das ich bey Gott im Himmel hab'.
Nach meinem Tod ist mir bereit
Des Himmels Freud u. Feyerkleid

Ich bin getauft in deinem Namen ,
Gott Vater, Sohn und heiliger Geist
Ich bin gezählt zu deinem Saamen ,

Zum Volk, das Dir geheiligt heißt.
O! welch ein Glück ward dadurch mein!
Herr, laß mich deßen würdig seyn!

Geschrieben und gebildet von Johannes Renninger.
1 8 4 1.

14. Birth and baptismal certificate. This certificate of the birth (September 3) and baptism (November 7, 1837) of Lewaina Bähr, in Colebrookdale Township, Berks County, was "written" by Johannes Renninger in 1841. In design the scrivener has followed the printed forms then in general use. The verses that appear on the certificate are transcribed and explained on page 16. This plate is about one third smaller than the original.

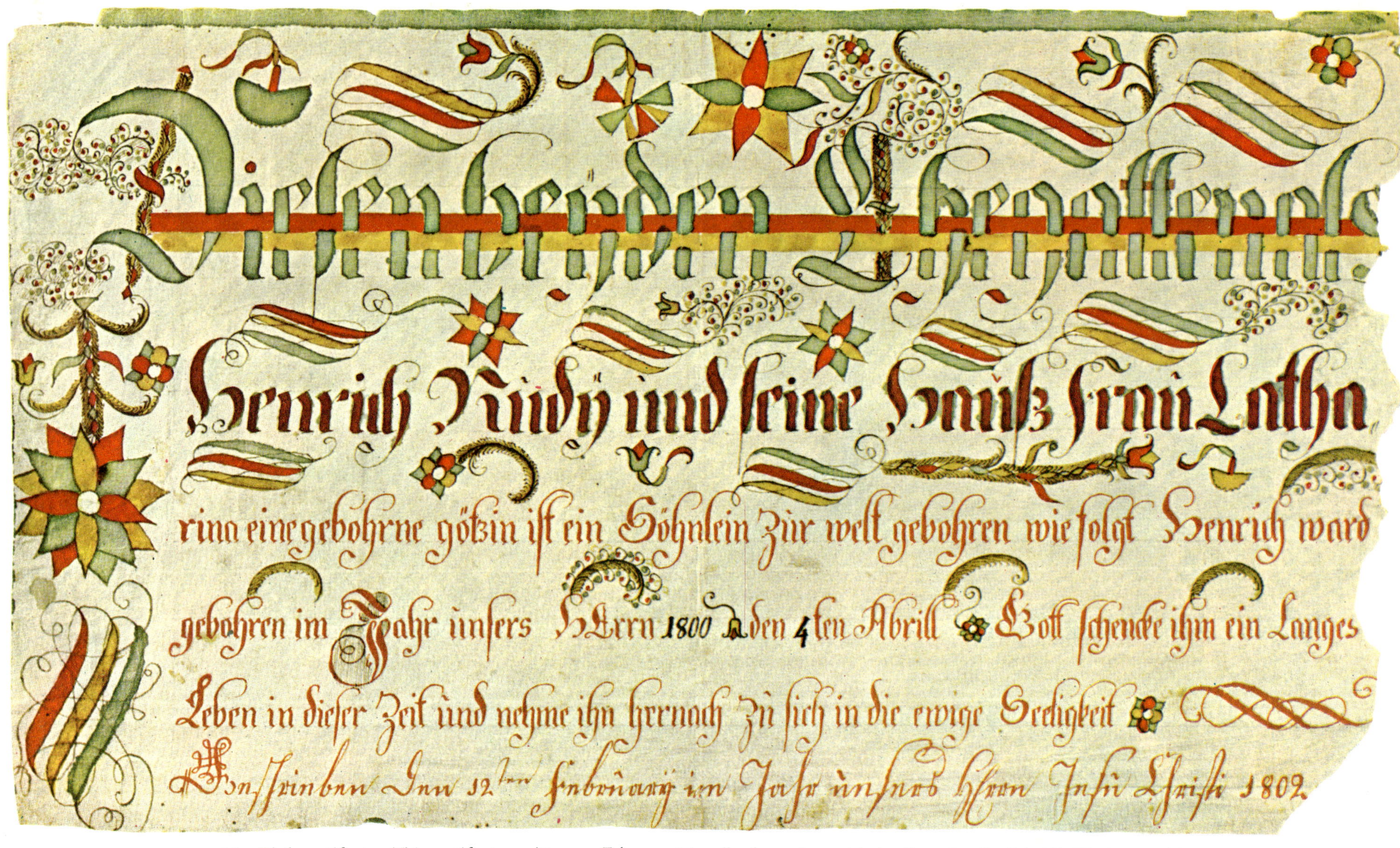

Diesen beyden Ehegatten als

Henrich Rudy und seine Hauß Frau Catha-

rina eine gebohrne götzin ist ein Söhnlein zur welt gebohren wie folgt Henrich ward

gebohren im Jahr unsers HErrn 1800 den 4ten Abrill Gott schencke ihm ein Langes

Leben in dieser Zeit und nehme ihn hernach zu sich in die ewige Seeligkeit

Geschrieben den 12ten Februarÿ im Jahr unsers Herrn Jesu Christi 1802

15. Birth certificate. This certificate, written on February 12, 1802, records the birth of Henrich Rudy on April 4, 1800. There is no reference to baptism. The text includes the prayer: "Gott schencke ihm ein Langes Leben in dieser Zeit und nehme ihn hernach zu sich in die ewige Seeligkeit" (God grant him long life in time and take him hereafter unto Himself into eternal happiness).

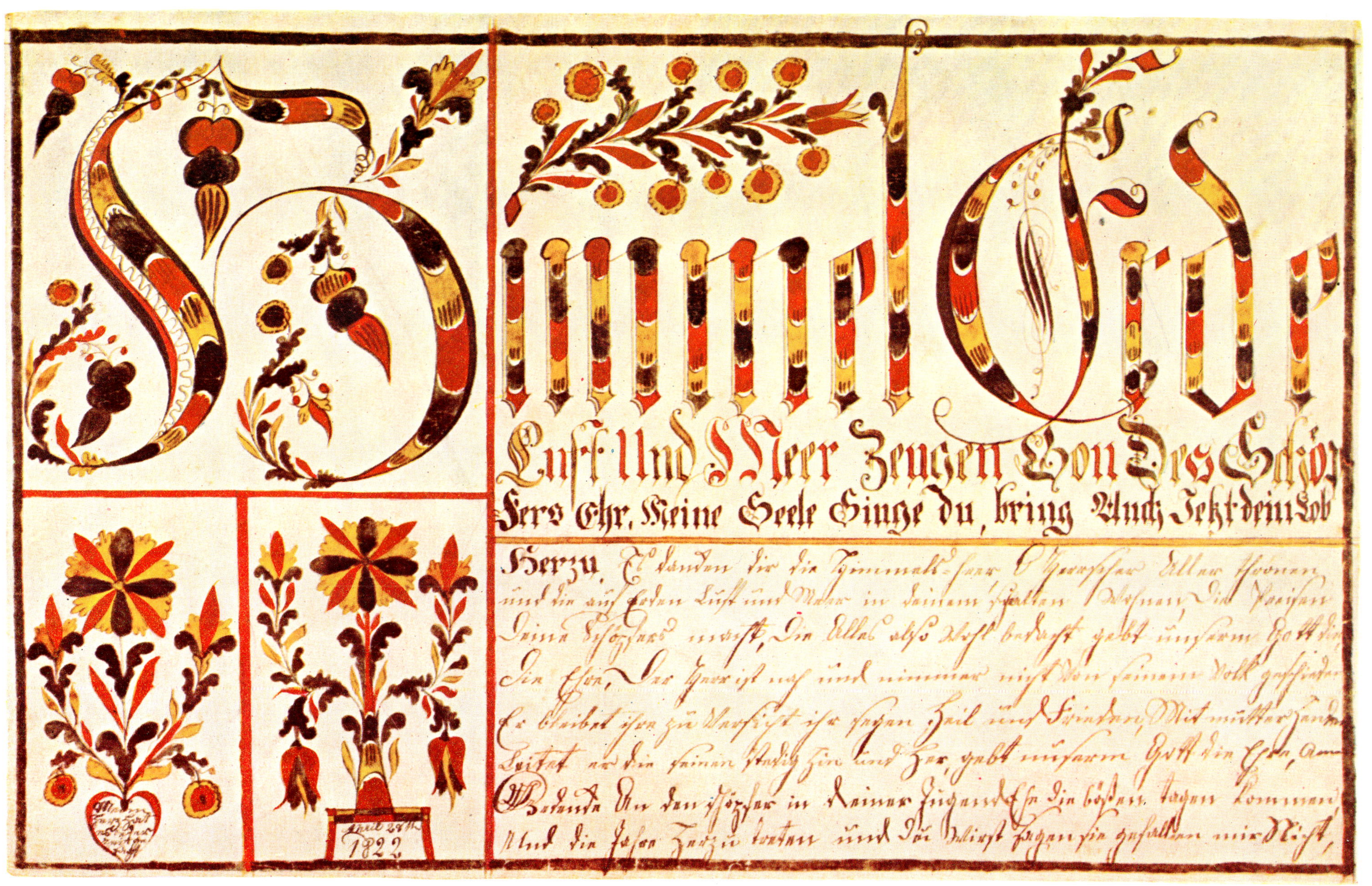

16. Confirmation certificate. It records that Catharine Heist was confirmed *(eingesegnet)* by Rev. Miller on May 11 and partook of Communion on May 12, 1822, Upper Milford Township, Lehigh County. The large text reads: "Himmel Erde Luft Und Meer/ Zeugen Von Des Schöpfers Ehr,/ Meine Seele Singe du,/ bring Auch Jetzt dein Lob Herzu" (Heaven, earth, air and sea/ Bear witness to the Creator's honor./ Sing, my soul,/ Add thy praise now too).

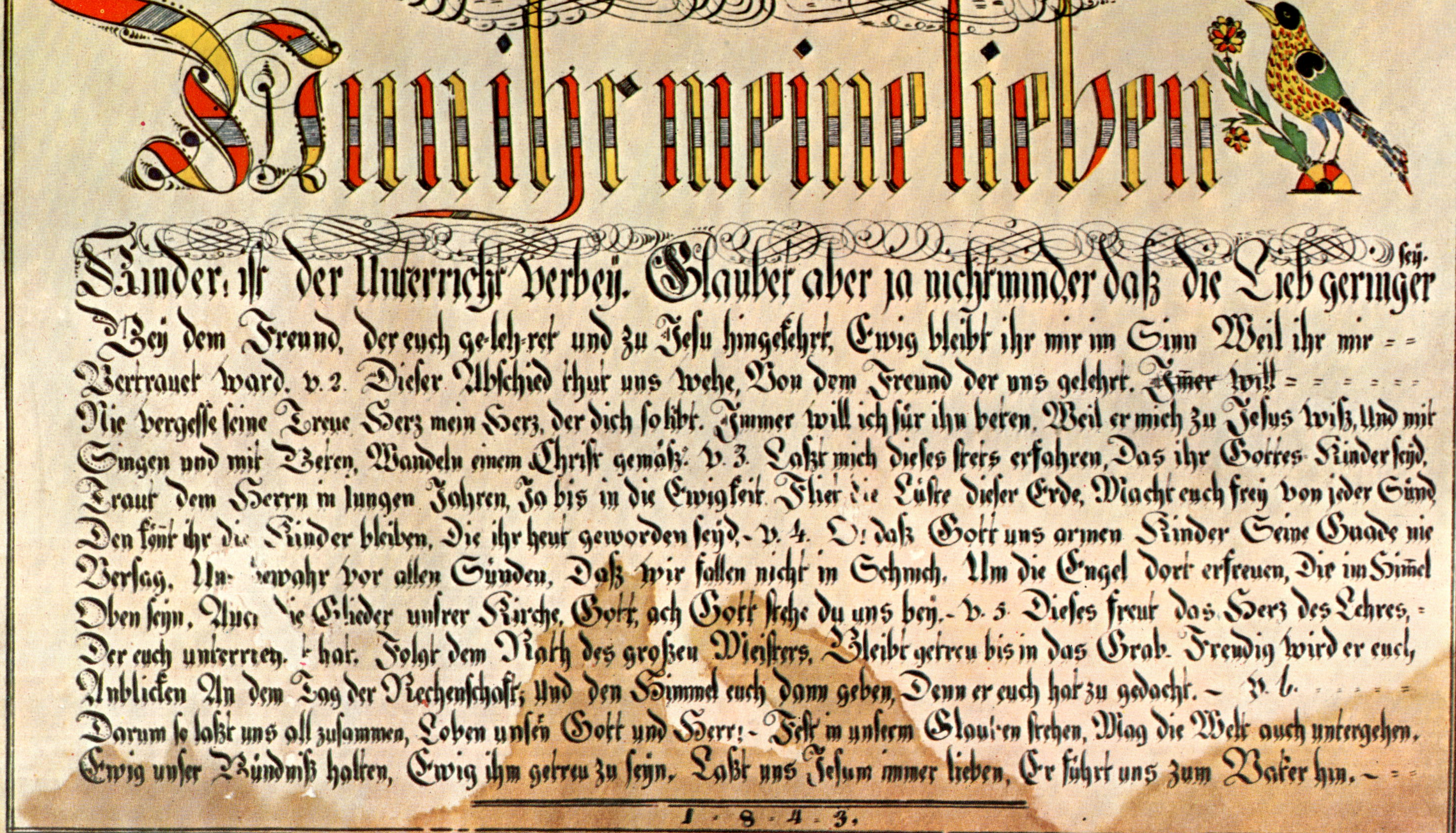

Nun ihr meine lieben

Kinder, ist der Unterricht verbey. Glaubet aber ja nicht minder daß die Lieb geringer sey.
Bey dem Freund, der euch ge-leh-ret und zu Jesu hingekehrt, Ewig bleibt ihr mir im Sinn Weil ihr mir = =
Vertrauet ward. v. 2. Dieser Abschied thut uns wehe, Von dem Freund der uns gelehrt. Jm̄er will = = = = = =
Nie vergesse seine Treue Herz mein Herz, der dich so libt. Jmmer will ich für ihn beten. Weil er mich zu Jesus wiß, Und mit
Singen und mit Beten, Wandeln einem Christ gemäß. v. 3. Laßt mich dieses stets erfahren, Das ihr Gottes Kinder seyd,
Traut dem Herrn in jungen Jahren, Ja bis in die Ewigkeit. Flier die Lüste dieser Erde, Macht euch frey von jeder Sünd
Den könt ihr die Kinder bleiben, Die ihr heut geworden seyd. - v. 4. O! daß Gott uns armen Kinder Seine Gnade nie
Versag. Un bewahr vor allen Sünden, Daß wir fallen nicht in Schmach. Um die Engel dort erfreuen, Die im Him̄el
Oben seyn, Auch die Glieder unsrer Kirche, Gott, ach Gott stehe du uns bey. - v. 5 Dieses freut das Herz des Lehres, =
Der euch unterrecht hat. Folgt dem Rath des großen Meisters, Bleibt getreu bis in das Grab. Freudig wird er euch
Anblicken An dem Tag der Rechenschaft; Und den Himmel euch dann geben, Denn er euch hat zu gedacht. - v. 6. = = = =
Darum so laßt uns all zusammen, Loben unsern Gott und Herr: - Fest in unserm Glauben stehen, Mag die Welt auch untergehen.
Ewig unser Bündniß halten, Ewig ihm getreu zu seyn. Laßt uns Jesum immer lieben, Er führt uns zum Vater hin. - = =

1 · 8 · 4 · 3.

17. Confirmation certificate, dated 1843 (place not indicated). The text begins: "Nun ihr meine lieben Kinder,/ ist der Unterricht verbey./ Glaubet aber ja nicht minder/ dasz die Lieb geringer sey" (Now, my dearly beloved children,/ The Instruction has ended./ But do not believe/ That my love has lessened).

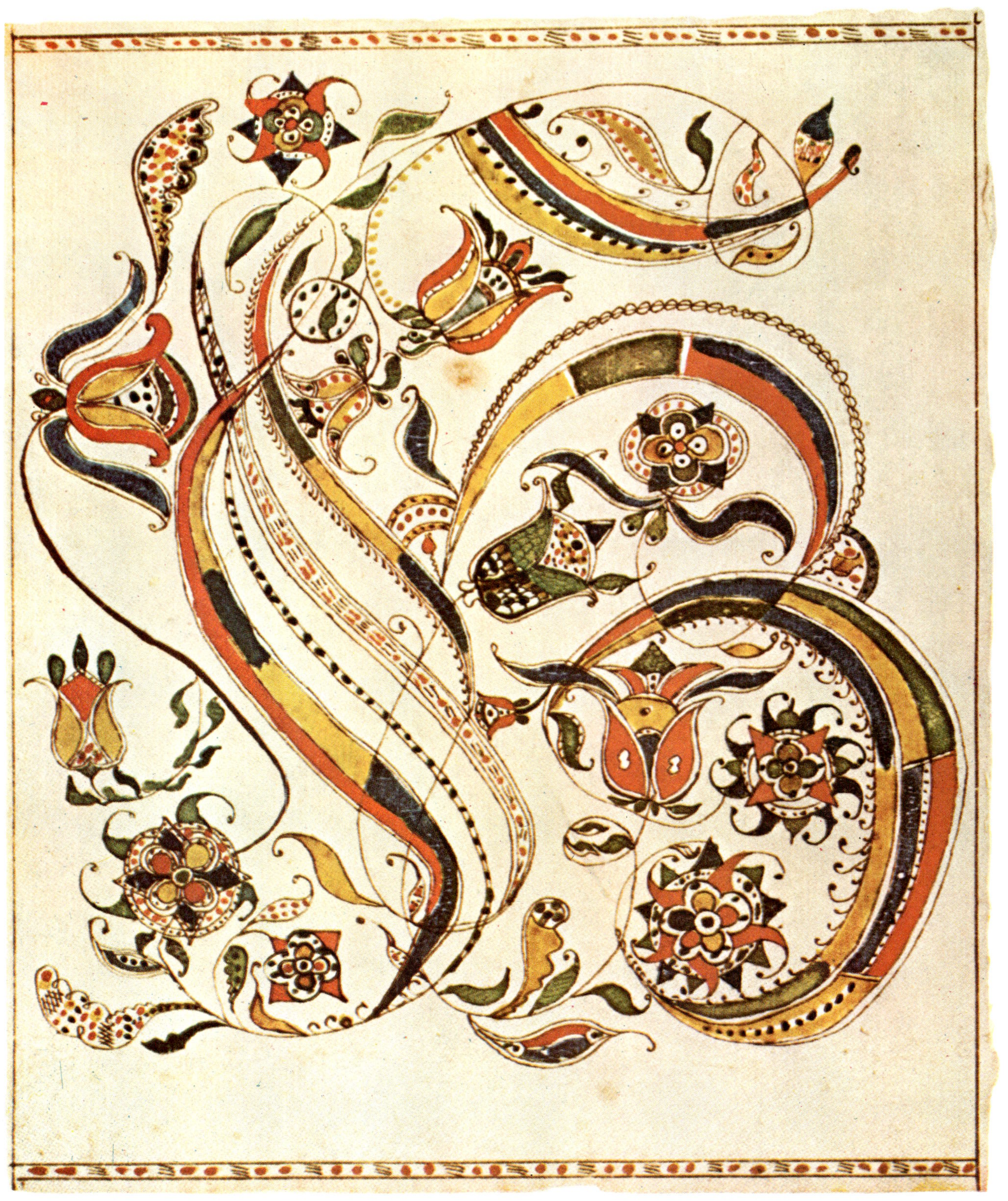

18. The letter B. This letter was a favorite with the illuminators of the Middle Ages. See page 36.

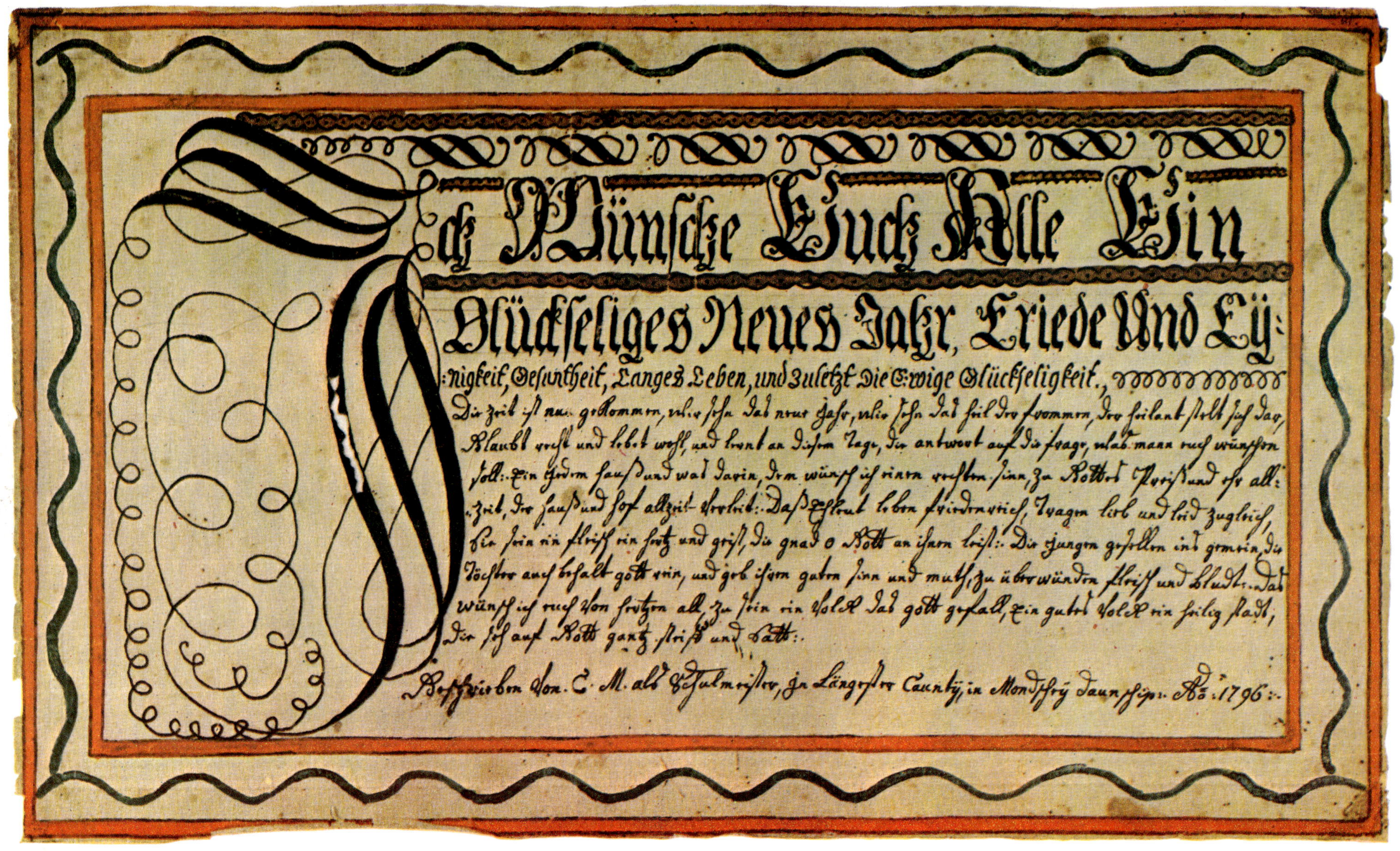

19. New Year's greeting. By C. M., schoolmaster in Mt. Joy, Lancaster County, 1796. The text begins: "Ich Wünsche Euch Alle Ein Glückseliges Neues Jahr, Friede Und Eynigkeit, Gesuntheit, Langes Leben, Und Zuletzt Die Ewige Glückseligkeit" (I wish you all a happy New Year, peace and unity, health, long life and finally, eternal happiness).

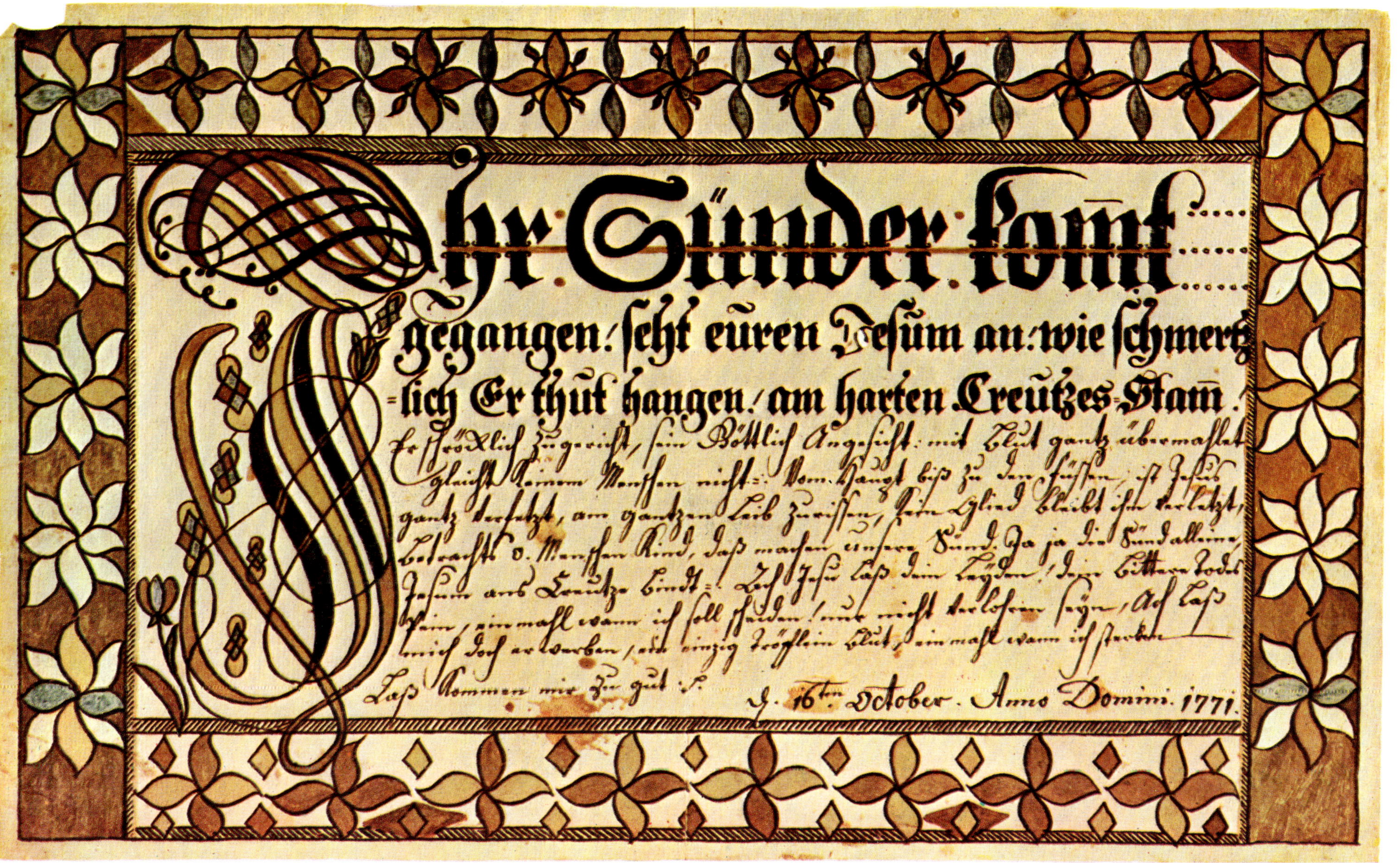

20. Christ on the Cross, a meditation, dated October 16, 1771. The text begins: "Ihr Sünder kom̄t gegangen/ seht euren Jesum an/ wie schmertzlich Er thut hangen/ am harten Creutzes-Stam̄" (Ye sinners, come,/ Behold your Jesus,/ How painfully He is hanging/ Upon the cruel cross). See page 33.

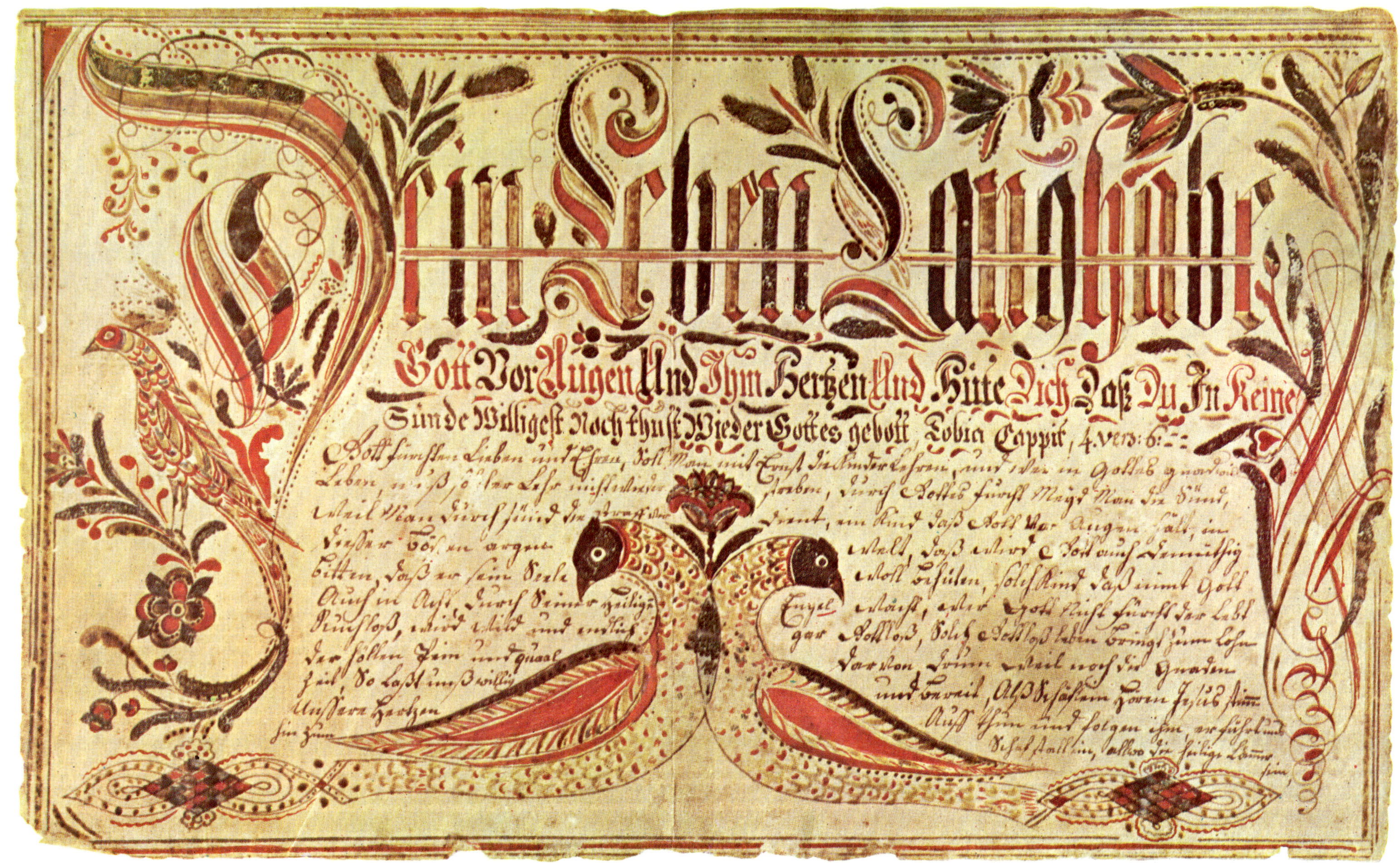

21. The instruction of youth. This manuscript is ascribed to Christopher Dock. The initial sentence in Fraktur is phrased upon a verse from the apocryphal Book of Tobit (4:6): "Dein Leben Lang habe Gott Vor Augen Und Ihm Hertzen Und Hüte Dich Dasz Du In Keine Sünde Willigest Noch thust Wieder Gottes gebott" (My son, be mindful of the Lord our God all thy days and let not thy will be set to sin or to transgress his commandments; do uprightly all thy life long, and follow not the ways of unrighteousness). The remainder of the text is translated on page 32.

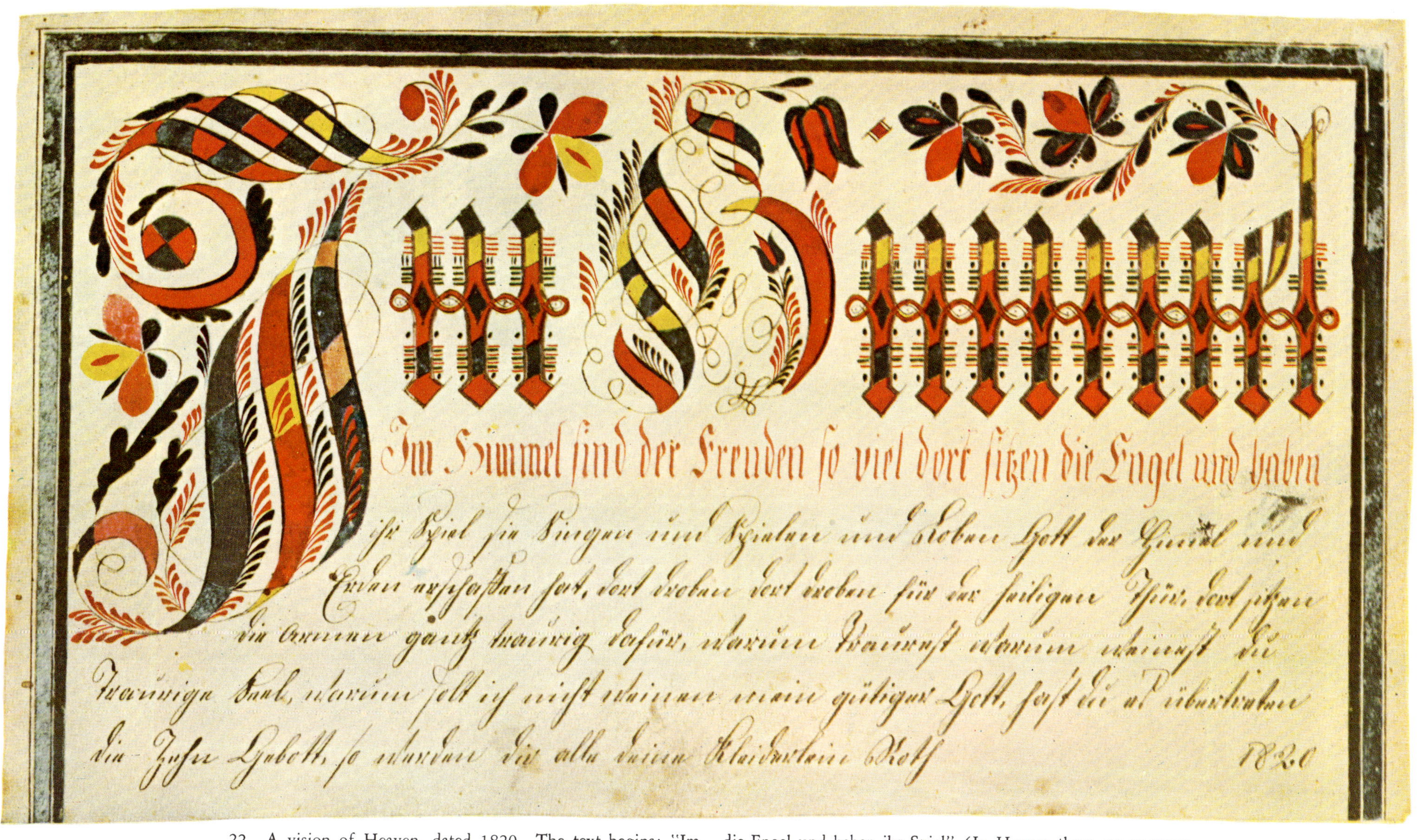

22. A vision of Heaven, dated 1820. The text begins: "Im Himmel — Im Himmel sind der Freuden so viel/ dort sitzen die Engel und haben ihr Spiel" (In Heaven there are so many joys./ There the angels sit and have their amusement).

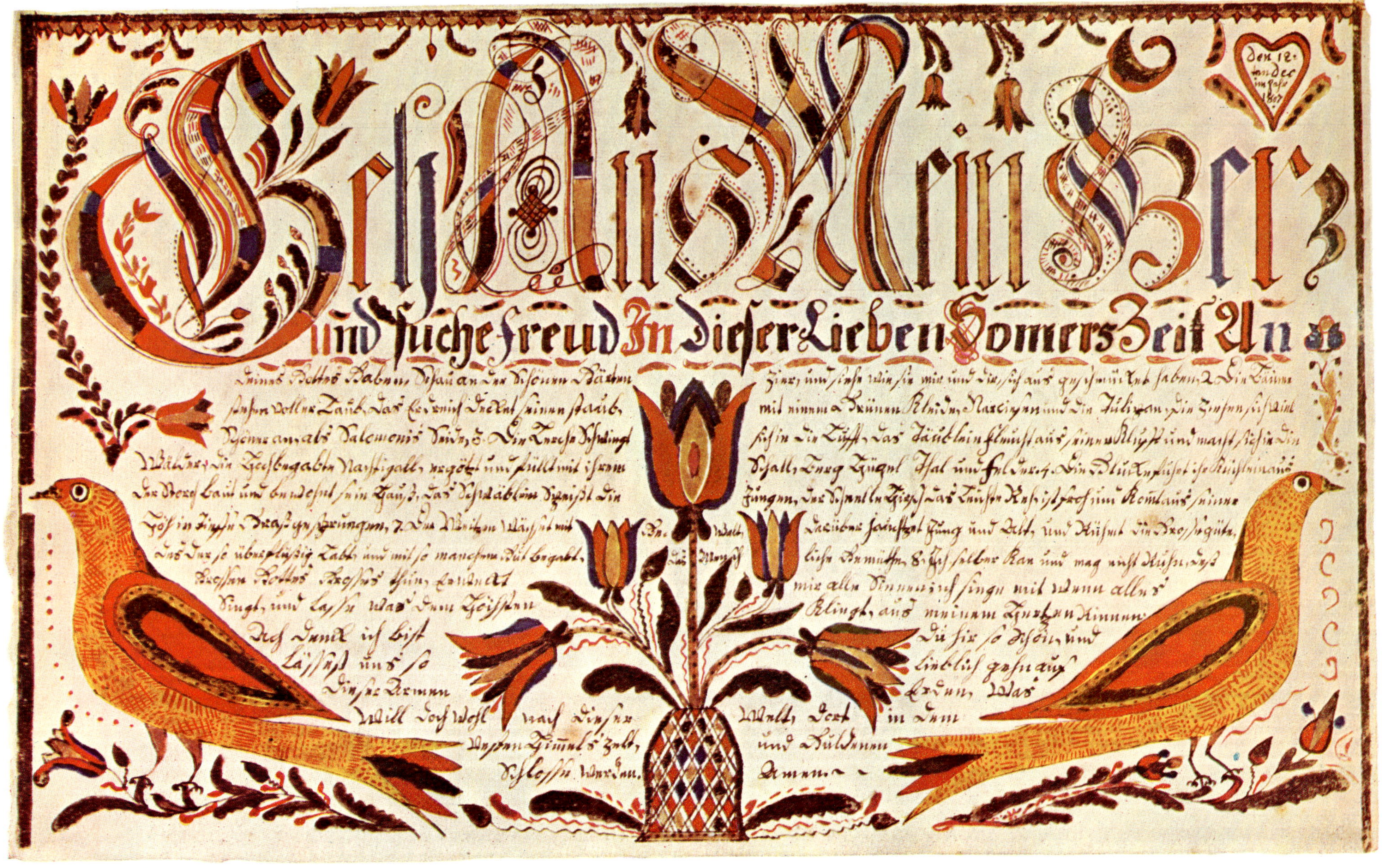

23. A song of summer, by Susanna Heebner, dated December 12, 1807 (see page 31). The text begins: "Geh Aus Mein Herz und suche freud/ In dieser Lieben Somers Zeit/ An Deines Gottes Gaben" (Go out, my heart, and seek joy/ during this beautiful summertime,/ in the gifts of your Lord).

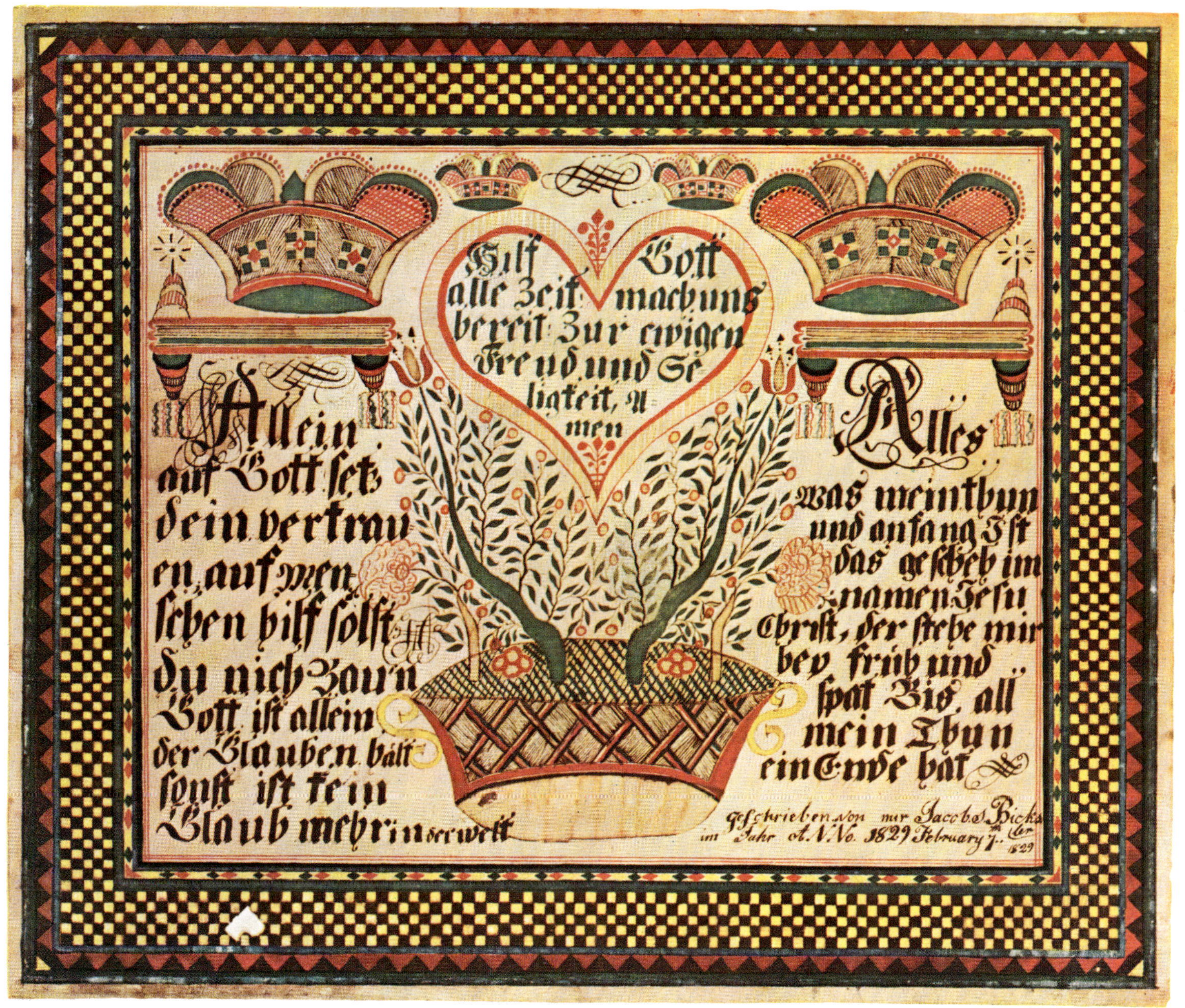

24. Religious precepts and prayer, by Jacob S. Bicksler, dated February 7, 1829. The prayer within the heart reads: "Hilf Gott alle Zeit/ mach uns bereit/ Zur ewigen Freud und Seligkeit/ Amen" (God help us ever,/ Make us ready/ For eternal joy/ And Bliss./ Amen).

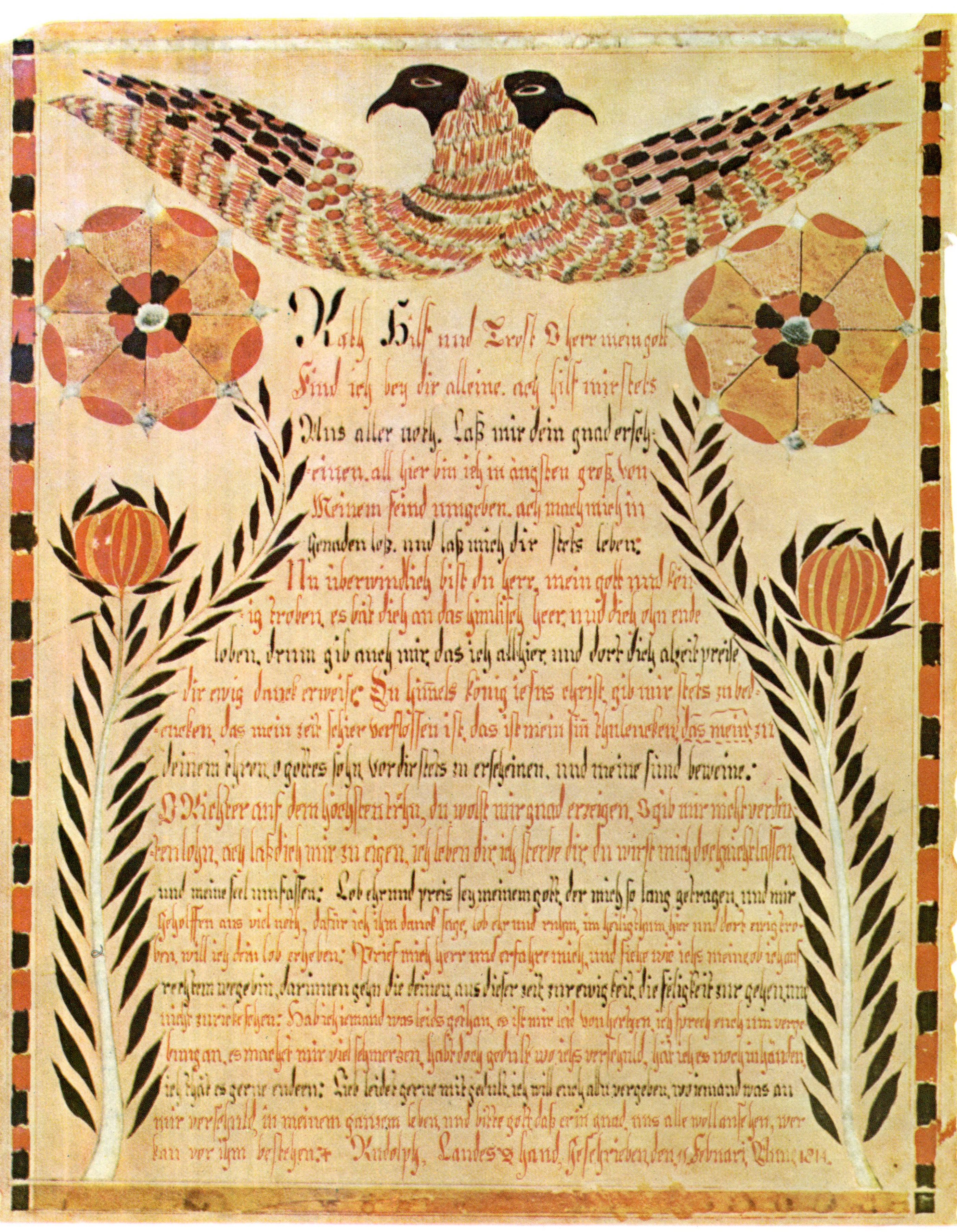

25. A prayer, by Rudolph Landes, dated February 11, 1814. The text begins: "Rath Hilf und Trost O herr mein gott/ Find ich bey dir alleine./ ach hilf mir stets Aus aller noth./ Lasz mir dein gnad erscheinen" (Counsel, aid and solace, O Lord my God,/ I find in Thee alone./ Ah, help me always in every distress,/ Let thy mercy appear before me).

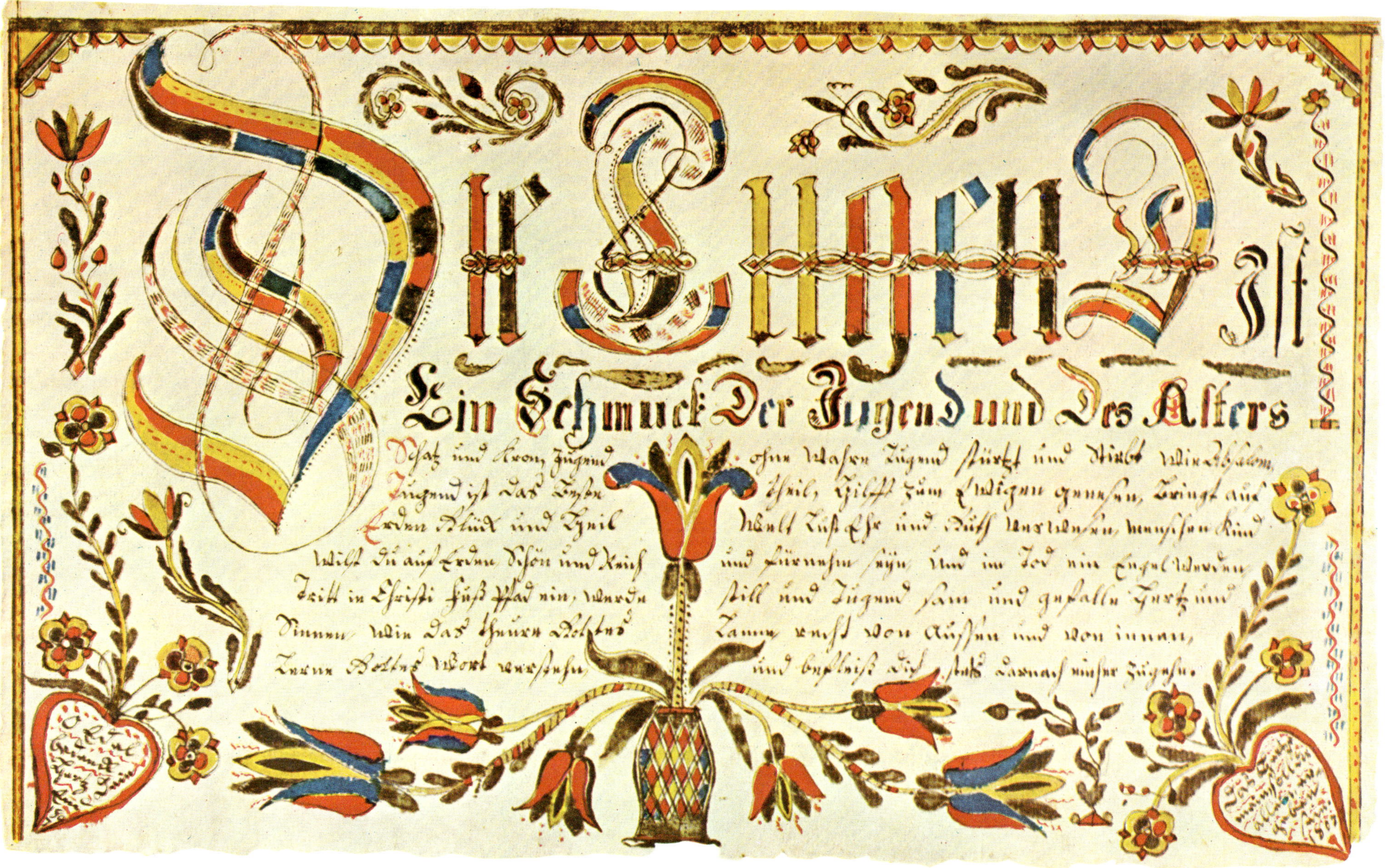

26. In praise of virtue, by Susanna Heebner, dated September 10, 1807. The text begins: "Die Tugend Ist Ein Schmuck Der Jugend und Des Alters" (Virtue is an adornment of youth and age). More of the text is translated on page 33.

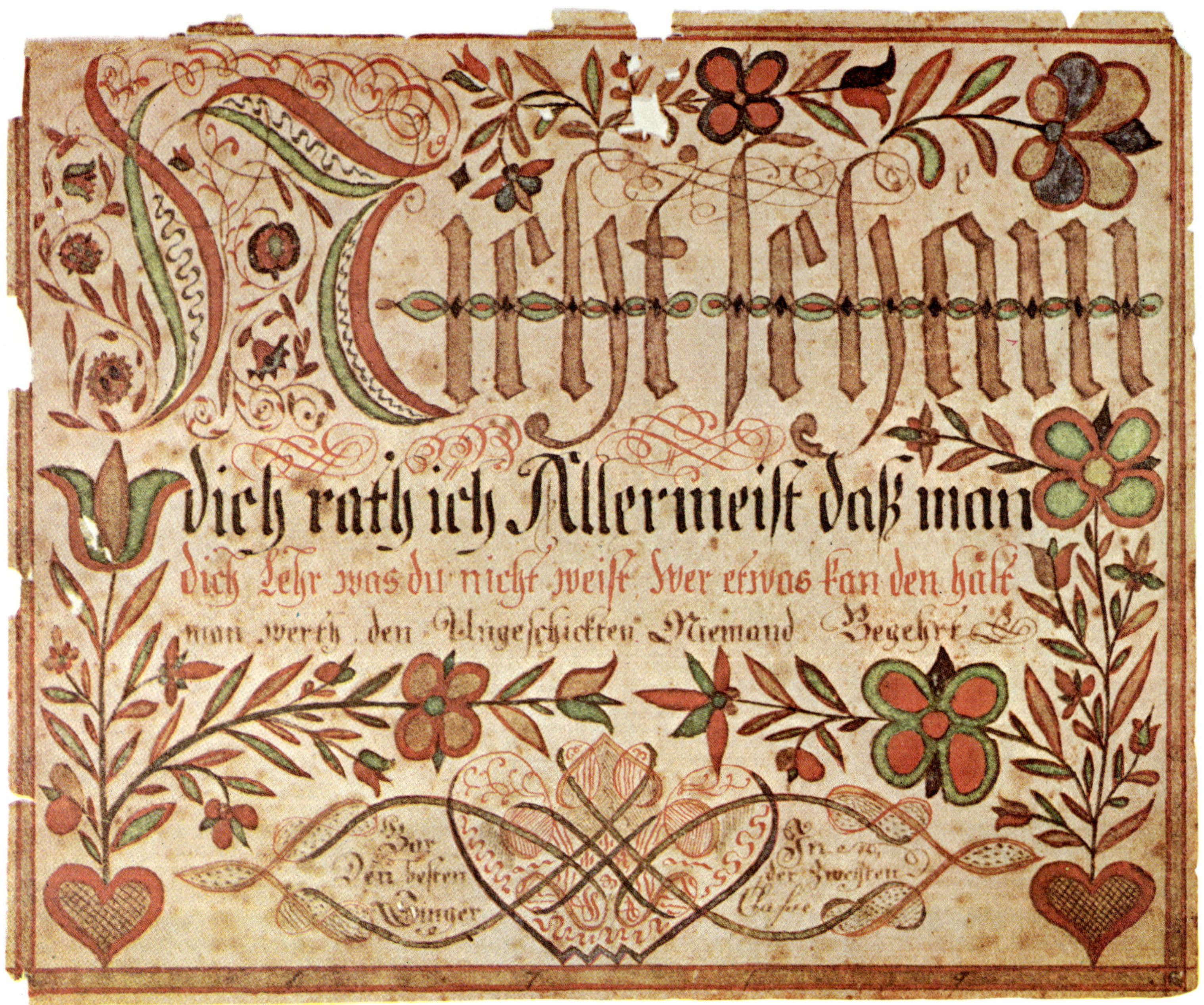

27. A reward of merit, dated 1779, for the best singer in the second class. The main text reads: "Nicht schäm dich rath ich Allermeist/ dasz man dich Lehr was du nicht weist/ Wer etwas kan den hält man werth/ den Ungeschickten Niemand Begehrt" (Do not be ashamed, I advise you most of all/ If someone teaches you what you do not know./ The man who knows something is esteemed,/ No one wants the man without skill).

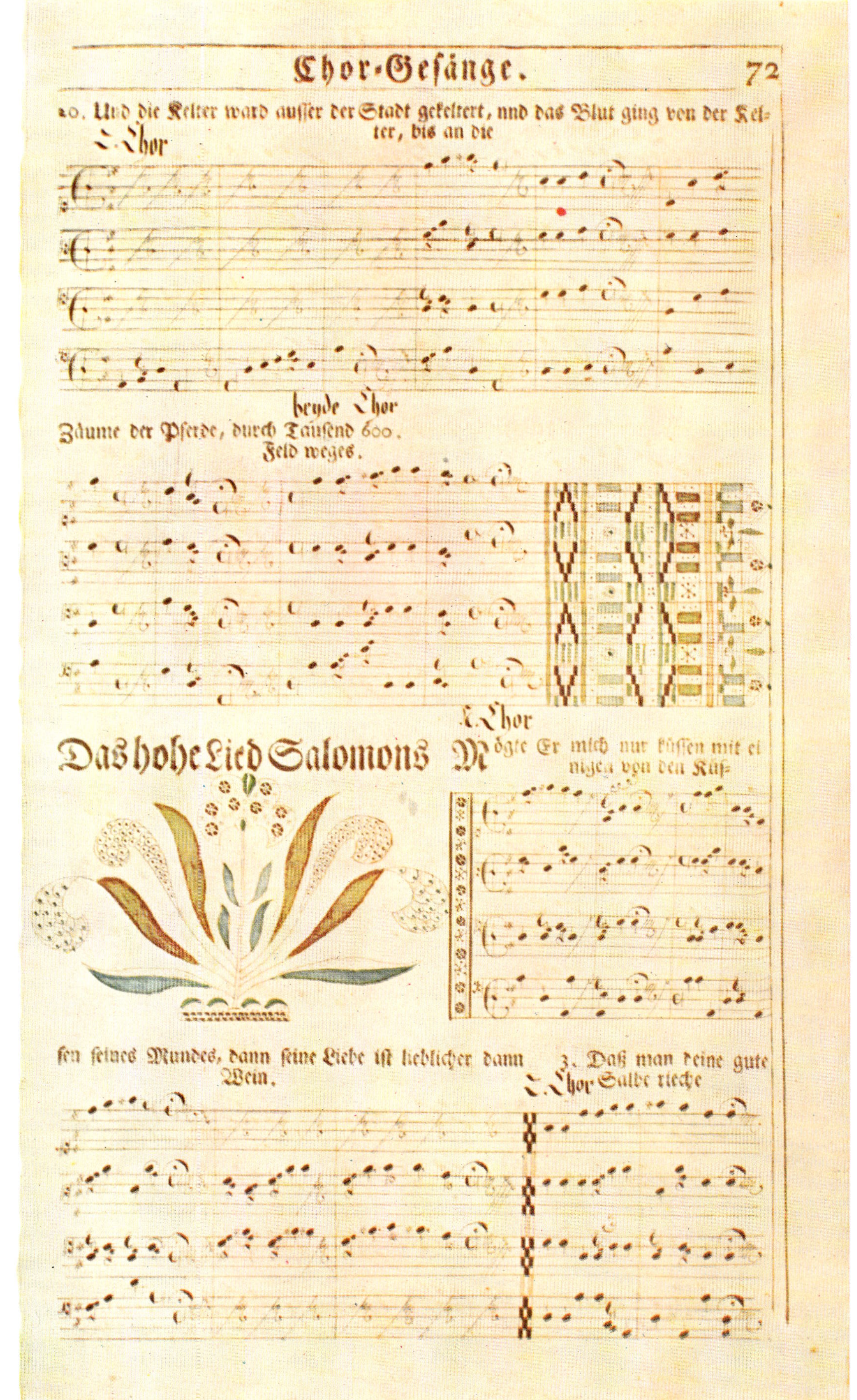

28. Illuminated book of music. A page from the *Paradiesisches Wunderspiel*. In this famous book of music, printed at Ephrata in 1754, the first line of each hymn and the staff are printed, and the notes and illuminations in color were added with quill and brush.

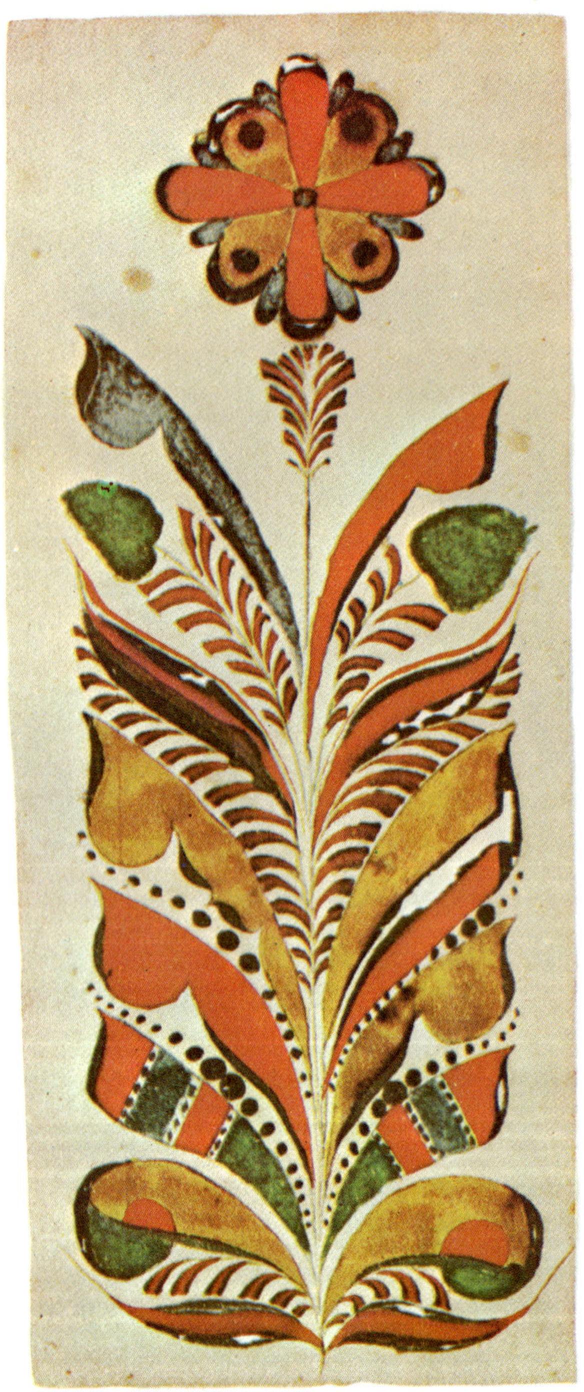

29. Color design.

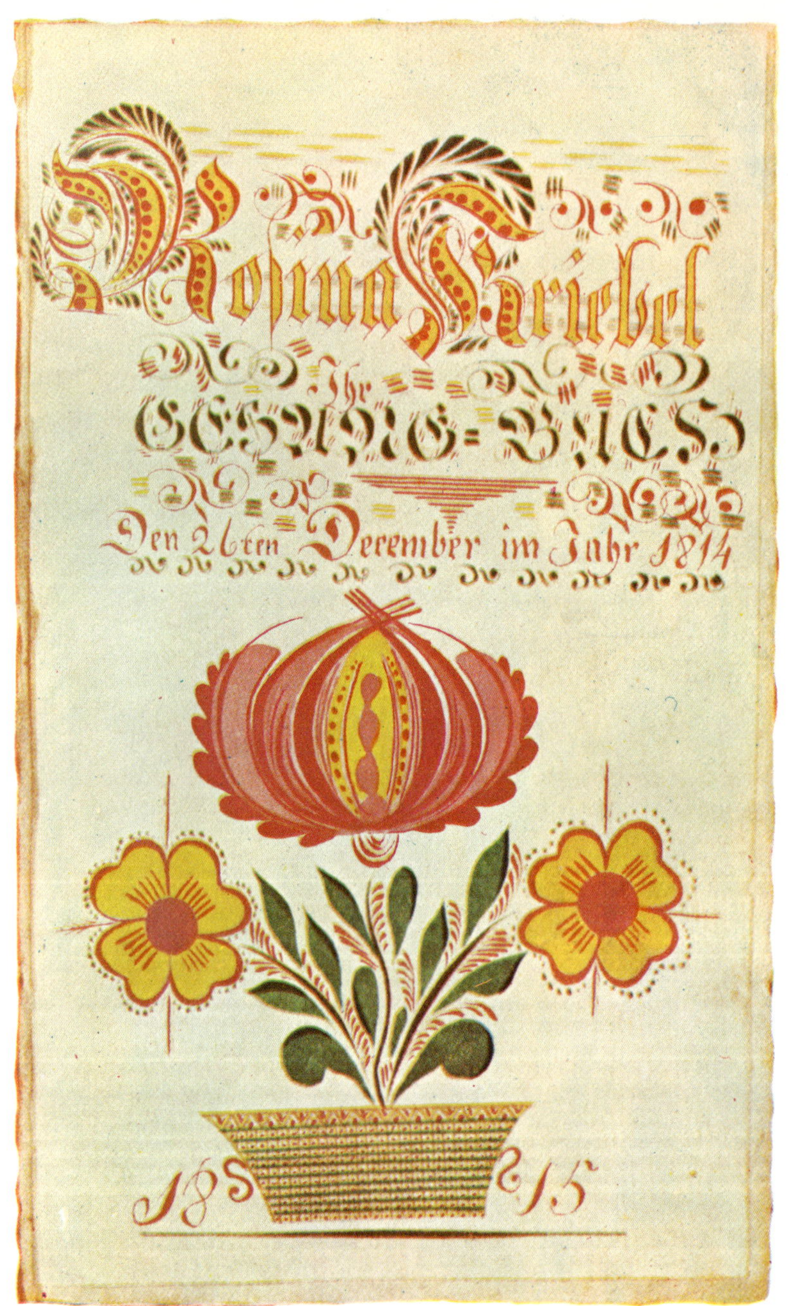

30. Book plate of Rosina Kriebel, "Ihr Gesang-Buch" (her songbook), in a Schwenkfelder hymnal. Dated December 26, 1814, and 1815.

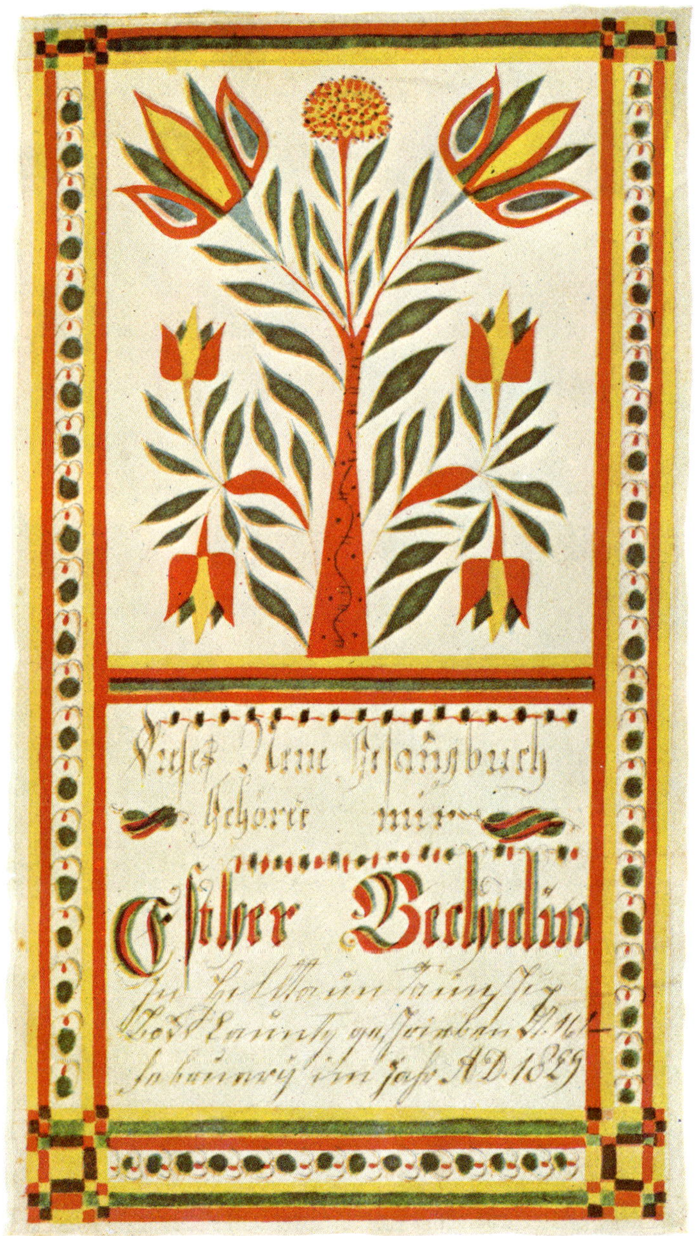

31. Book plate, dated 1829, of Esther Bechtel, in a Mennonite hymnal.

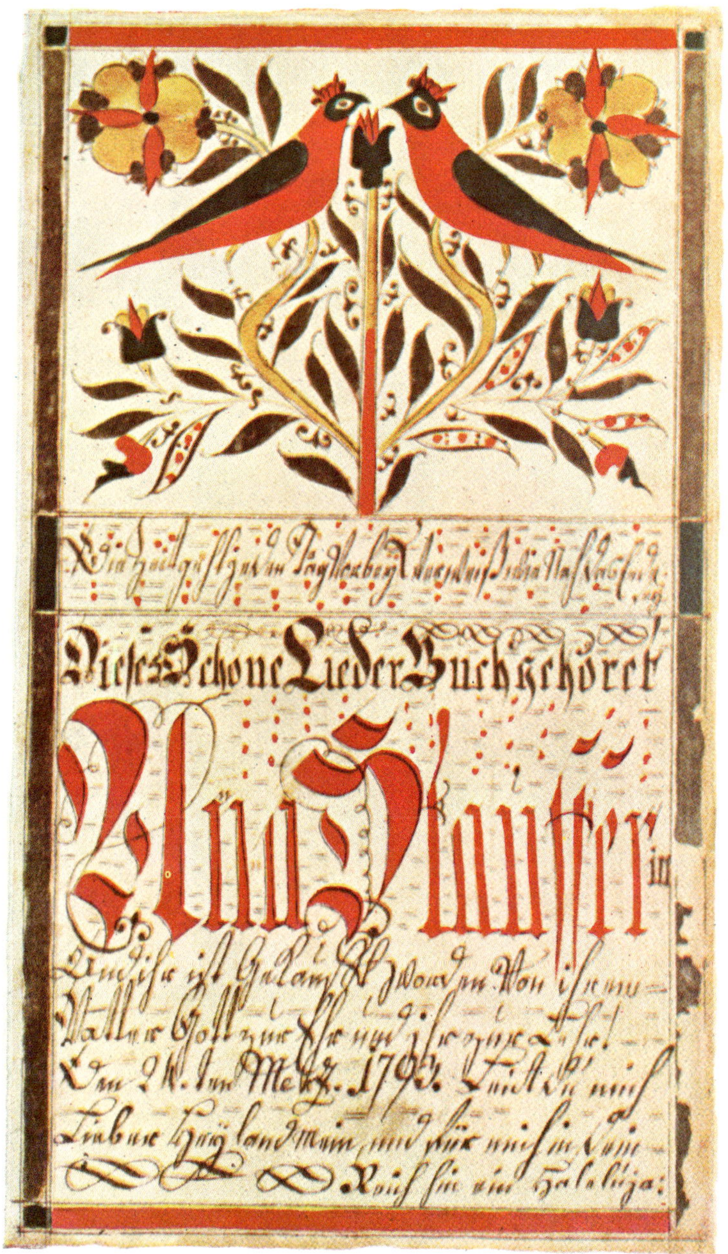

32. Book plate, dated 1793, of Anna Stauffer, in a Mennonite hymnal.

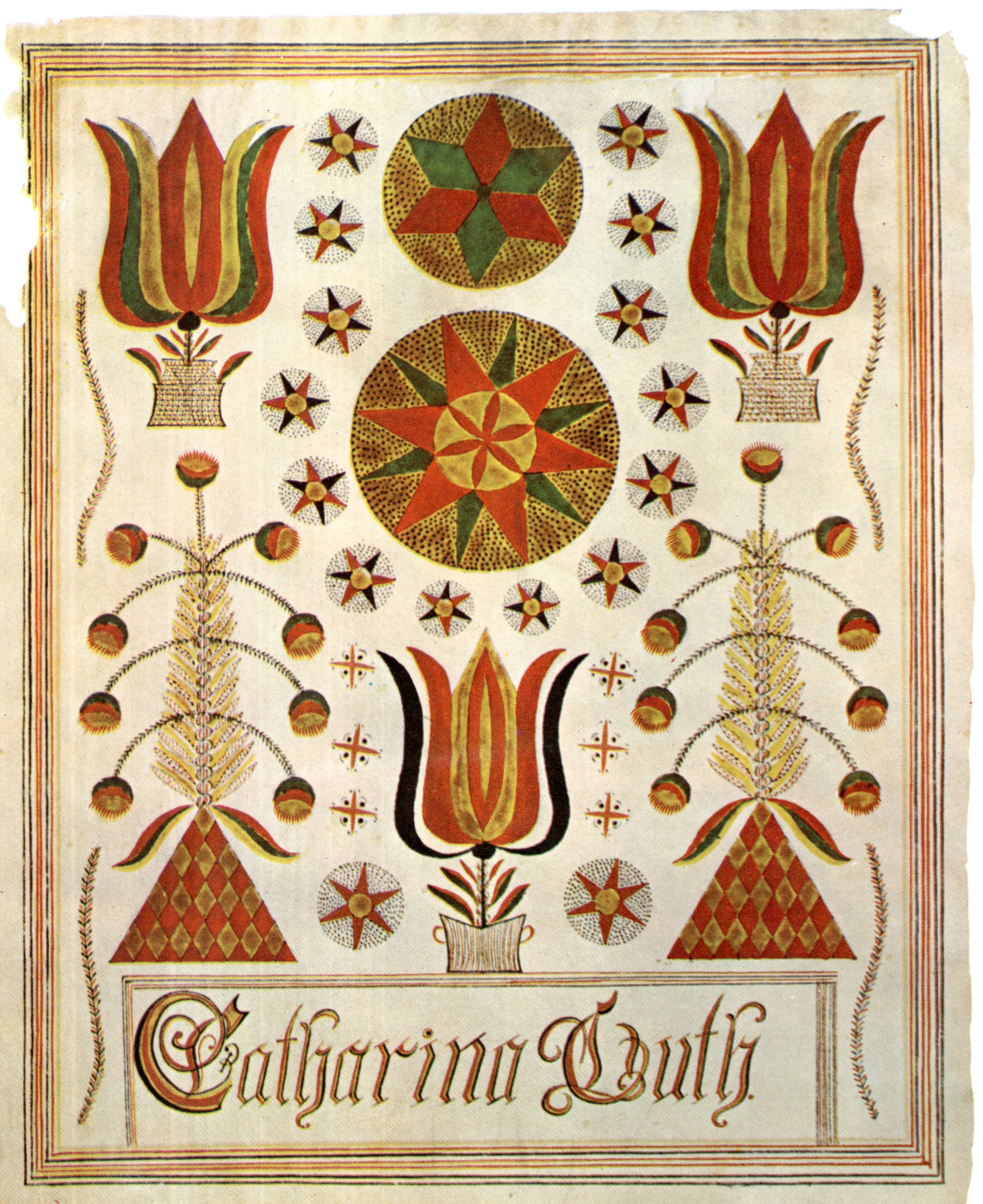

33. Book plate from the Bible of Catharina Gùth.

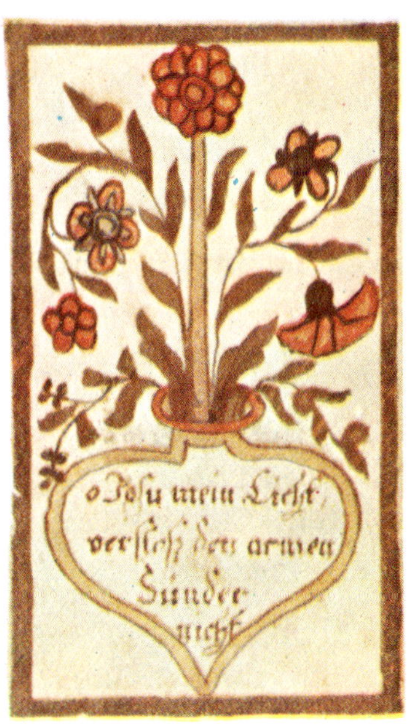

34. Prayer: "O Jesu mein Licht,/ verstosz den armen Sünder nicht" (O Jesus, my light,/ Cast not the poor sinner out of thy sight).

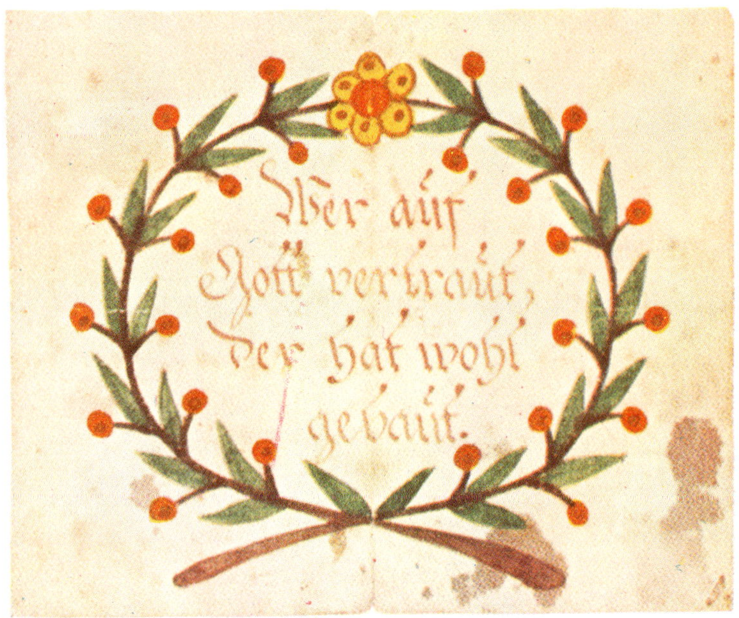

35. Color design with house motto. Text and translation on page 23.

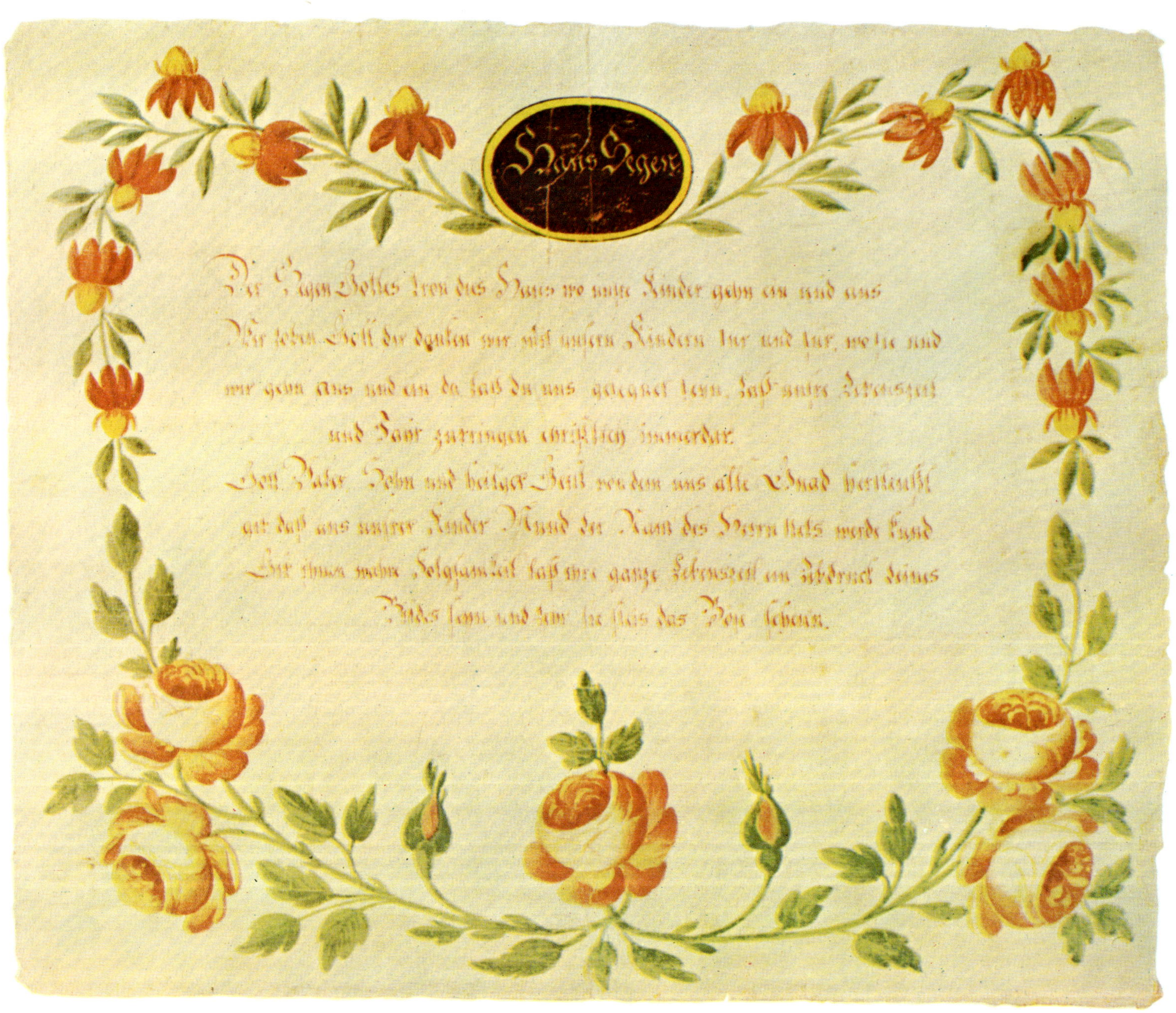

36. *Haus Segen* (house blessing). Full text and translation on pages 22 and 23. This plate is about one third smaller than the original.

Geistlicher Irrgarten,

Mit vier Gnadenbrunnen, dadurch kürzlich angedeutet werden: erstlich, die vier Ströme des Paradieses, und der glückselige Zustand des Menschen vor dem Fall. 2tens, durch das verkehrte Lesen werden angemerket, die vielen und mancherley Kümmernisse und Drangsale dieses Lebens. 3tens, daß er aber an gleichem Ort anfängt und endet, zeiget: Gleichwie alles Wasser aus dem Meer, und wieder in dasselbe fliesset: Also der Mensch, sobald er in diese Welt geboren, mit seinem Leib wieder zu seiner Mutter der Erde eilet. Die Seele aber soll ein jeder Christ GOtt täglich durch Buße, Glauben und Gebät aufopfern, bis sie auch zu GOtt ihrem Ursprung und in seine völlige Geniessung und Besitzung gelangen kann. 4tens, Endlich wird angewiesen, wie der Mensch durch den Satan zur Sünde gereizet und zu Fall gebracht worden, dadurch die ganze Natur des Menschen verderbet ist: deshalben, wie ein irrendes Schaaf herum wandert, bis GOtt seinen Gnaden-Arm über ihn ausstrecket, und durch seinen Heiligen Geist aus dem göttlichen Gesez als einem geistlichen Spiegel überzeuget, ihm seine Augen öffnet, daß er sein tiefes Elend sehen und erkennen kann, mit Verlangen daraus erlöset zu werden. Darauf er zu Gott rufet, der ihm rathet, und durch sein heiliges Wort auf Christum weiset, und durch den wahren Glauben an Christum JEsum auf die rechte Straße des Lebens gebracht wird, und also glückselig heraus kömmt, zur ewigen Seligkeit. GOTT leite alles zum Preis seines Heiligen Namens, und zum Guten seiner Gemeine.

Ich bin wie ein verirret und verloren Schaaf, suche deinen

Knecht: dann ich vergesse deiner Gebote nicht. Ps. 119.

Wir giengen alle in der Irre wie Schafe, ein jeglicher sahe auf seinen Weg;

aber der HErr warf unser aller Sünde auf Ihn. Es. 63, 6. Ezech. 34, 4.

37. Spiritual Labyrinth. Religious precepts, in varying forms and puzzling arrangements, circulated among the Pennsylvania Germans prior to 1840. Explanation of text on page 25. About one third smaller than the original printed broadside.

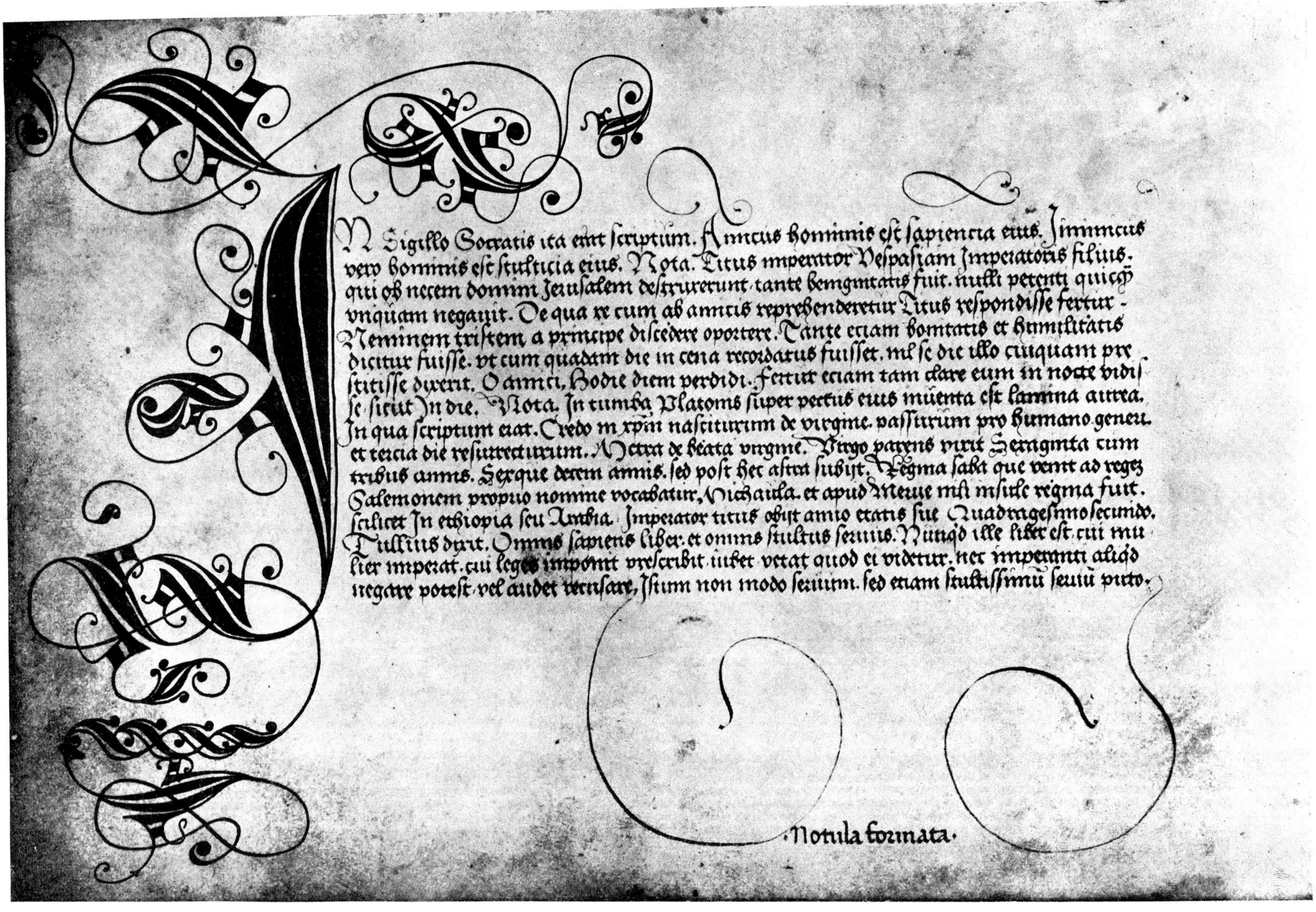

In sigillo Socratis ita erat scriptum. Amicus hominis est sapiencia eius. Inimicus
vero hominis est stulticia eius. Nota. Titus imperator Vespasiani Imperatoris filius.
qui ob necem domini Jerusalem destruxerunt. tante benignitatis fuit. nulli petenti quicq̄
vnquam negavit. De qua re cum ab amicis reprehenderetur Titus respondisse fertur.
Neminem tristem a principe discedere oportere. Tante eciam bonitatis et humilitatis
dicitur fuisse. vt cum quadam die in cena recordatus fuisset. nil se die illo cuiquam pre
stitisse dixerit. O amici. Hodie diem perdidi. Fertur eciam tam clare eum in nocte vidis
se sicut In die. Nota. In tumba Platonis super pectus eius inuenta est lamina aurea.
In qua scriptum erat. Credo in xp̄m nasciturum de virgine. passurum pro humano genere.
et tercia die resurrecturum. Metra de beata virgine. Virgo parens vixit Sexaginta cum
tribus annis. Sexque decem annis. sed post hec astra subijt. Regina saba que venit ad regez
Salemonem proprio nomine vocabatur. Nicaula. et apud Meroe insule regina fuit.
scilicet In ethiopia seu Arabia. Imperator titus obijt anno etatis sue Quadragesimo secundo.
Tullius dixit. Omnis sapiens liber. et omnis stultus seruus. Nunq̄d ille liber est. cui mu
lier imperat. cui leges imponit prescribit iubet vetat quod ei videtur. nec imperanti aliq̄d
negare potest vel audet recusare. Istum non modo seruum. sed etiam stultissimū seruū puto.

Notula formata.

38. Vorschrift. A suggestive prototype from a manuscript in Fraktur entitled *Hundert schriften von ainer hand der kaine ist wie die ander* (A Hundred Scripts, All Different from One Another, Written by One Hand), written by Leonhard Wagner in 1507. The Latin text mentions examples of wisdom, piety and goodness in antiquity.